Background to Britain

Background to Britain

M D Munro Mackenzie

L J Westwood

M

First published 1965
Reprinted 1966, 1967 (twice), 1968, 1970,
1971 (twice), 1972, 1974, 1976, 1977
New edition 1978
Reprinted 1978, 1981, 1982
New edition 1983
Reprinted 1984 (twice)

Published by *Macmillan Publishers Ltd*
London and Basingstoke
Associated companies and representatives in Accra,
Auckland, Delhi, Dublin, Gaborone, Hamburg, Harare,
Hong Kong, Kuala Lumpur, Lagos, Manzini, Melbourne,
Mexico City, Nairobi, New York, Singapore, Tokyo.

ISBN 0 333 36119 9

Printed in Hong Kong

Preface

In this new, revised edition of *Background to Britain* we have not, apart from deleting some now inappropriate chapters and replacing them with new ones, made any very substantial alterations. We have not done so because the sales of the book and the comments of its users have testified to the fact that it has been fulfilling—as we hoped it would—a very useful function in its original form. What we *have* done is to make a number of emendations and additions in order to bring the content of the chapters more up to date, and also to correct statements which the passage of time has rendered inaccurate or irrelevant. In doing this, we have incorporated suggestions from teachers who regularly use the book.

The purpose of the book, as stated in the original preface, is that of providing short reading passages which have been specially written to give the student some idea, without going into too much detail, of various aspects of life in Britain today. Each passage can be read and the vocabulary in it studied in the course of a single lesson of average duration. The matter is suitable for use by students of an intermediate stage, *i.e.* the type of student who is preparing for the Cambridge First Certificate in English for Foreign Students, or for those in the middle forms of schools.

Each passage is followed by a number of exercises. Apart from providing work on the vocabulary of the text, these deal with grammatical matters to be found in it, or arising from it. Questions on the content of the passage are also set. The exercises may be worked through orally in class or they may be used for homework. Each series of exercises includes a subject for an essay. Most of the passages will be found suitable for practice in summary.

We are gratified that this little book has been found helpful by our colleagues and their students. We hope that now, in its revised form, its useful life will be considerably extended.

Acknowledgements

The authors and publishers wish to acknowledge the following photograph sources. They have made every effort to trace the copyright holders of all the illustrations, but where they have failed to do so they will be pleased to make the necessary arrangement at the first opportunity.

Aerofilms, 39, 131
Allied Breweries, 36, 37
Chris J. Arthur, 29
Peter Baker, 33, 138, 139
Barnabys Picture Library, 5, 38
Basingstoke District Hospital, 143
British Broadcasting Corporation, 28, 53
British Steel Corporation, 165
British Tourist Authority, 8, 13, 16, 36, 37, 61, 69, 73, 81, 103, 105, 114, 117, 121, 126
Camera Press, 113, 114, 134
J. Allan Cash, 34, 49, 61b, 92, 96, 97, 146, 167
Cheese Bureau, 111
Chichester Festival Theatre, 30
Bruce Coleman, 98
Courage, 36, 37
English National Opera Co., 30
Foyles, 24
H.M.S.O., 131a
Keystone Press Agency, 43, 47, 48, 106, 156
Kwikform Ltd, 77
Littlewoods Pools, 56, 57
The Mansell Collection, 127
Massey Ferguson, 159
Paramount Picture Corporation, 150
Post Office, 122
Graham Reed, 12, 84, 85
Royal Shakespeare Theatre, 30
Kenneth Scowen, iii
By kind permission of Richard Slessor, 114
Tate Gallery, 102a
Tate Gallery/Mrs Wyndham Lewis, 102b
Thames Television, 20
Welsh Folk Museum, 74

Contents

As others see us

We are rarely able to see those who are very close to us as they really are because of our readiness to accept their faults and accentuate their virtues. The same is equally true when we come to look at ourselves. It is very difficult for anybody to be objective about his own character. Yet it is very good for us to try to be so from time to time. As the Scottish poet Robert Burns put it:

O wad[1] some Pow'r the giftie[2] gie[3] us
To see oursels[4] as others see us!
It wad frae[5] mony[6] a blunder free us
And foolish notion.

What Burns says about individuals is equally true of nations. Every country tends to accept its own way of life as being the normal one and to praise or criticize others as they are similar to or different from it. And unfortunately, our picture of the people and the way of life of other countries is often a distorted one.

Here is a great argument in favour of foreign travel and learning foreign languages. It is only by travelling in, or living in, a country and getting to know its inhabitants and their language, that one can find out what a country and its people are really like. And how different the knowledge one gains this way frequently turns out to be from the second-hand information gathered from other sources! How often we find that the foreigners whom we thought to be such different people from ourselves are not so very different after all!

Differences between peoples do, of course, exist and, one hopes, will always continue to do so. The world will be a dull place indeed when all the different nationalities behave exactly alike, and some people might say that we are rapidly approaching this state of affairs. With almost the whole of Western Europe belonging to the European Economic Community and the increasing standardisation that this entails, plus the much greater rapidity and ease of travel, there might seem some truth in this—at least as far as Europe is concerned. However this may be, at least the greater ease of travel today has revealed to more people than ever before that the Englishman or Frenchman or German is not some different kind of animal from themselves.

Yes, travel does broaden the mind. And learning the language

[1]would [2]gift [3]give [4]ourselves [5]from [6]many

and culture of another nation does liberalise one's outlook. It is to be hoped that more and more of the ordinary people in all countries will have the opportunity to do both things in the future. But when people travel they should be open to new experiences. Too often English people abroad create their own community, keeping to English ways of life no matter where they might be.

A   Vocabulary

1   What does *objective* mean? What is its opposite?
2   Find a synonym for *readiness*.
3   Find an antonym of *virtue* (not *fault*).
4   What do you do when you *accentuate* something?
5   What sort of picture is a *distorted* one?
6   Explain the meaning of the phrase *turns out to be*.
7   Give a synonym for *blunder*.
8   What is *second-hand* information?
9   Find two or three synonyms for *dull*.
10 What is the opposite of *rapidly*?
11 Explain the meaning of *broaden* in the phrase 'travel does broaden the mind.'

B   Questions on 'As others see us'

1   What do we all find difficult to do?
2   What sort of picture do we tend to have of those who are close to us, and why?
3   What did the poet Burns consider to be the advantages of seeing ourselves as others see us?
4   What sort of attitude does each country have towards its own way of life?
5   Give an important argument in favour of foreign travel.
6   What is the only way of finding out what a foreign country is really like?
7   What is the opinion of some people concerning the differences between different nations?
8   What effect does travel have on one's mind?

C Grammar

1 Put the following sentences into reported speech.
   a Which of these roads will take me into town?
   b Run and tell father that supper is ready.
   c How pleasant it is just to sit and do nothing!
   d How many goals did you score when you played football this afternoon?
   e Put your books away tidily when you leave the room.
   f Leave your things here when you go and I will look after them.
   g Next week I shall be starting my holidays.
   h Please go away!
2 Insert a suitable interrogative pronoun or adjective in the following sentences.
   a . . . . coat is this? Yours or mine?
   b . . . . country do you come from?
   c . . . . is wrong with you?
   d . . . . is the name of this flower?
   e . . . . answer did he give to my question?
   f . . . . bus goes to London Bridge?
   g . . . . sort of shoes are those you're wearing?
   h . . . . is the matter?

D The adjective formed from the word 'England' is 'English'. Give the adjectives formed from the following countries.

Germany, France, Italy, Sweden, Poland, Russia, Finland, Scotland, China, Spain, India, Wales, Japan, Ireland, Switzerland.

E Write an essay on your first impressions of any foreign country and its people.

The Cockney

Almost everyone who has heard of London has heard of the term 'Cockney'. Strictly speaking, in order to call oneself a Cockney one should have been born 'within the sound of Bow bells', that is to say within the sound of the bells of the church of St Mary-le-Bow, which stands nearly in the centre of the City of London. But, in fact, all London's citizens who were born and bred in the city may call themselves Cockneys if they wish. However, the term is generally reserved for the Londoner with a 'Cockney accent'.

The Cockney accent is not a particularly pleasant or melodious one, and the Cockney's distortion of the English language is such that the foreigner often finds it impossible to understand the speaker until his ear has become acclimatised to the peculiar tones. The principal characteristics of the Cockney accent consist in a general slurring of consonants (the aspirate aitch is often ignored) and a distortion of vowel sounds. The best known example of Cockney speech in modern English literature is that of Eliza Doolittle, the heroine of Bernard Shaw's play, *Pygmalion* and of the musical adapted from it, *My Fair Lady*.

But if Cockney speech is unpleasant, the Cockney himself is usually far from being so. The average Cockney is distinguished by his quick wit, his ready sense of humour, his ability to 'carry on' under unusual or difficult conditions and by his willingness to be of help if he can. The Cockney's humour is often satirical but it is never vicious; he is very ready to laugh at other people's peculiarities but he is equally ready to laugh at his own. He often makes jokes under the most difficult conditions, a quality that was very apparent during World War II. This rather lugubrious type of humour is well exemplified by the title of an old Cockney music-hall song: 'Ain't It Grand To Be Blooming Well Dead'.

Nowadays, as the tempo of life in big cities grows ever faster (although the Cockney opposes this process when he can), the opportunities for the Cockney to exercise his wit and humour diminish. But if one keeps one's ears open on buses, in railway stations, in street markets and similar places, it will soon become evident that the spirit of Cockney humour is still very much alive, although the old Cockney pronunciation is less common than hitherto.

Most people who call themselves Cockneys usually do so with some pride. And, by and large, they are justified.

Most colourful of London's Cockneys are the Pearly Kings and Queens –
so-called because their traditional costumes are decorated with hundreds of
pearl buttons.

Many Cockney expressions seem mysterious because they are
based on 'rhyming slang', where the original words are replaced by
words that rhyme with them.
For example:

apples and pears	= stairs	Uncle Ned	= bed
mince pies	= eyes	bees and honey	= money
plates of meat	= feet	custard and jelly	= telly (television)

6   The Cockney

A   Vocabulary

1   Find an alternative for the word *bred*.
2   What does *melodious* mean? Name three sounds which you consider to be particularly melodious.
3   What is the literal meaning of *acclimatised*? In what sense is it used in the passage?
4   Find a synonym for *principal* in the phrase 'principal characteristics'.
5   What is the *aspirate aitch*?
6   How would you define *slurred* speech?
7   What is *satirical* humour?
8   Find an alternative for *lugubrious*.
9   What is the *tempo* of life?
10   What does a thing do when it *diminishes*?

B   Questions on 'The Cockney'

1   What is the strict definition of a Cockney?
2   Where is the church of St Mary-le-Bow situated?
3   What is the City of London?
4   What are the main characteristics of the Cockney accent?
5   What are the characteristics of the Cockney himself?
6   When were these characteristics very noticeable?
7   Why are the opportunities for the exercise of Cockney wit and humour diminishing?
8   Where might one still expect to hear examples of Cockney wit?
9   How do the Cockneys feel about their name?

C   Grammar

1   Put the adverbs of manner (shown in brackets) in the correct place in each of the following sentences.
    a The Cockney speaks English. (unmelodiously)
    b He worked for many weeks. (hard)
    c The boxer hit his opponent on the chin. (hard)

d The boys refused to obey their teacher. (stubbornly)
e He refused to see me as I was late. (angrily)
2 Add the necessary question-tag in the following sentences
(e.g. It's a nice day, *isn't it*?).
  a I am clever .... ?
  b You must go now .... ?
  c You will be back soon .... ?
  d She dresses badly .... ?
  e Tom is going home .... ?
  f You haven't seen Joan .... ?
  g Owls eat mice .... ?
  h You'd do it if you could .... ?
3 Give the past tense and the past and present participles of
these verbs.
write, ring, grow, speak, wear, show, tear, sing, throw

D The following sentences show different uses of the verb
'to take'. Put suitable words in the spaces allowed.

1 The dentist had to take .... my bad tooth.
2 Take the quotation .... in your notebooks.
3 The plane was due to take .... at five o'clock.
4 He took a coin .... his pocket for the telephone call.
5 If one is bored it is a good idea to take .... a hobby of
some kind.
6 Will you take .... my work for a little while? I need a rest.
7 I did not take .... the man when I first met him, and my
dislike has increased since.
8 Waiter, take this soup .... ; it is cold.

E Write an essay on any group of people who, like the
Cockney, have characteristics peculiar to themselves.

Piccadilly Circus

It is difficult to say what is the real centre of London, but many people would choose Piccadilly Circus. This is because it is not only central but also the heart of London's entertainment world. Within a few hundred yards of it we find most of London's best-known theatres and cinemas, the most famous restaurants and the most luxurious night-clubs.

In the middle of Piccadilly Circus there is a statue said to be of Eros, the god of love. Few people know that it really represents the Angel of Christian Charity. This statue is the first that was ever cast in aluminium. On Cup Final night and New Year's Eve it is boarded up to prevent over-enthusiastic revellers from climbing onto it. (The Cup Final is the match which decides the winning football team.)

The buildings around the Circus are rather nondescript, though

Theatres and neon lights at Piccadilly.

some of them are large and quite imposing. Many of them are decorated with bright neon signs advertising goods and entertainments; Piccadilly Circus at night is a colourful sight.

Underneath Piccadilly Circus there is an important tube station with escalators leading down to two different lines. The ticket-hall, which is just below street-level, is a vast circular hall with showcases, hired by various stores, let into the walls. There are entrances from all the main streets that converge at the Circus.

It is particularly in the evening that Piccadilly Circus is thronged with people going to the theatre or the cinema, or perhaps to a restaurant. Many others have come for an evening stroll; they will probably have a cup of coffee or a glass of beer before they go home. The crowd is a motley one, for it is composed of people of many nationalities. The peoples of the British Commonwealth are well represented, as there are many Indians, Pakistanis, West Indians and Africans in London; they are either working here or studying. Some of them wear their national dress. Many foreign visitors mingle with the crowd, some from the Continent, some from more distant places. It is interesting to try to identify different nationalities by their style and type of clothing. This is no longer as easy as it used to be. The atmosphere is distinctly cosmopolitan, and one hears around one a great variety of languages. It has been said that if you listen carefully, you may even hear English!

A   Vocabulary

1   What is meant by the word 'Circus' in Piccadilly Circus?
2   What is aluminium?
3   What is an escalator?
4   Name three sorts of public entertainment.
5   What is meant by the word diverge?
6   What is the difference between to hear and to listen?
7   When we go for a stroll, are we in a hurry?
8   Explain the difference in meaning between cloths and clothing.
9   When an Englishman speaks of the Cup Final, to what is he referring?
10   What do we call a man who shoots with bow and arrow? What is the name of the sport he practises?

B   Questions on 'Piccadilly Circus'

1 Why is Piccadilly Circus called the centre of London?
2 What is there in the middle of the Circus?
3 Why is it sometimes boarded up?
4 What makes Piccadilly Circus colourful at night?
5 What is there underneath the Circus?
6 How do people get down to the tube stations?
7 Why are there so many people in the Circus in the evening?
8 What sort of people does one find in the crowds in the Circus?
9 What interesting activity is no longer as easy as it used to be? Why?
10 Does one hear only English in Piccadilly Circus?

C   Grammar

1 Give the abstract nouns corresponding to the following adjectives.
famous, luxurious, enthusiastic, important, various
2 Insert the correct prepositions in the following sentences.
   a The square was thronged . . . . people.
   b The salad was composed . . . . lettuce, tomatoes and cucumber.
   c Several detectives mingled . . . . the shoppers.
   d . . . . night the lights illuminate a gay scene.
   e Let's go . . . . a walk.
   f The square was full . . . people.
   g The building was decorated . . . . coloured lights.
   h He went out . . . . the evening.
   i The statue is made . . . . aluminium.
   j There will be a ball . . . . New Year's Eve.
3 Give the past tense, and the past and present participles of these verbs.
meet, find, hold, lead, sing
4 Give the comparative and superlative forms of these adjectives.
famous, luxurious, large, distinct, careful

D   Complete the following sentences.

1   He can not only speak English but also . . . .
2   He can speak not only English but also . . . .
3   He can neither speak English nor . . . .
4   He can speak neither English nor . . . .
5   To get there, you can travel either . . . . or . . . .
6   . . . . do you want to go to, the theatre or . . . . ?
7   We can either go out for a meal or . . . . , just as you like.
8   Make up your mind or I . . . .
9   You can either come with me or . . . .
10 I don't know whether . . . . or to . . . .

E   Pronunciation

1   In the word *climb* the *b* is not pronounced. Give other words,
ending in a silent *b,* for the following.
    a the young of a sheep
    b a place where someone is buried
    c a weapon that explodes with great violence
    d something with which to arrange one's hair
    e an arm or a leg
2   Mark the strong (i.e. stressed) syllables in the words
given below. (Use an acute accent, e.g. 'cathedral'—cathédral'.)
luxurious, Piccadilly, Piccadilly Circus, converge, atmosphere,
restaurant, monument, escalator, nationality, particular

F   Write an essay on the main square (or the market square)
of your own town or village.

Lunch in Town

Most people who work in London get a break of about an hour for lunch. As they mostly live too far from home to go back there for lunch, they are obliged to make other arrangements for their midday meal.

Many large firms have a canteen on the premises for their employees. In such canteens the food served is plain but adequate, and although there is some variety of choice, the number of dishes is usually small. The employees themselves fetch their dishes from a counter at which they are served. There they can find a tray on which to carry their knives, forks, spoons, plates, cups, saucers, and, of course, their food. A meal in a canteen is inexpensive and may consist of soup, fish and chips or meat and two vegetables, with fruit or a pudding of some sort as dessert. Some firms that do not run a canteen provide their staff with luncheon-vouchers, which many restaurants will accept in place of money.

As there are so many people at work in London, there are numerous cafés and restaurants in every area that is not purely residential. A meal may cost anything from a modest sum to quite

Some firms provide a bar where staff can get lunch.

a few pounds, depending on the restaurant and the food chosen. Moreover, one can generally get a meal, or at least a snack, in a pub ('pub' is the usual word for a public house, a place where people go to drink such things as beer and spirits). A number of well-known caterers run popular cafés in practically every district of London. In many of these cafés there is self-service—there are no waiters or waitresses. Instead the customers help themselves and pay at a cash-desk before going to their tables. In recent years there has also been a big increase in the number of 'take away' food shops of all kinds.

Many employees do not bother to go out to lunch. They bring their own sandwiches, and perhaps an apple or a bun, with which they have a cup of tea, probably made in the office. This method has the advantages of being cheap and of saving time in getting to a restaurant and queueing up there. In summer, many people go out and sit on a bench in a park or public square, and eat their sandwiches there, giving the crumbs to the sparrows and pigeons. They are also often able to listen to lunch-time concerts and plays.

A lunch-time concert in a London park

14   Lunch in Town

A   Vocabulary

1   An employee is a person given employment. What do we call the person who provides the employment?

2   The feminine of *waiter* is . . . .

3   Give another word for 'practically' in the phrase 'in practically every district of London'.

4   What is the opposite of 'expensive'? (use a prefix) Find, in the text, another word that is the opposite.

5   What adjective describes a part of a town where people live rather than work?

6   Give two meanings of the word 'dish'.

7   What is the word that describes all the employees of a firm, school, hospital, etc.?

8   We put food on a plate, but our cup on a . . . .

9   What do we call the last course of a meal?

10   What is a *luncheon-voucher*?

B   Questions on 'Lunch in Town'

1   How long do most business people get for lunch in London?

2   Why do people not go home for lunch?

3   What sort of food can one get in a staff canteen?

4   Does a meal in a canteen cost much?

5   Why are there so many restaurants in London?

6   What do customers have to do in many popular cafés?

7   What do many employees bring with them for lunch?

8   What are the advantages of a quick meal in the office? And the disadvantages?

9   What happens to the crumbs that people drop when they eat out-of-doors in London?

C   Grammar

1   Give the past tense, past participle and present participle of these verbs.

live, cost, get, run, bring, make, queue, go, sit, choose

2   Give the adverbs corresponding to the following.
large, plain, usual, general, probable

3   Insert *much* or *many* as required in the following sentences.
    a . . . . people like apples.
    b Too . . . . food is bad for you.
    c There are . . . . sparrows here.
    d He caught . . . . fish.
    e A simple meal shouldn't cost . . . .

4   Insert the correct preposition in the following sentences.
    a My friend works . . . . London.
    b They will provide you . . . . luncheon-vouchers.
    c The result will depend . . . . your work.
    d It sells . . . . thirty pence a pound.
    e Tom was sitting . . . . a chair . . . . the park.
    f You should share your good luck . . . . . your friends.
    g You will have to pay . . . . least eighteen pence.

D   Complete the following sentences.

1   Although the food was plain, ...
2   However hungry you may be, ...
3   Although there was a wide variety of dishes, ...
4   Although the sky is cloudy, ...
5   I must have something to eat, although . . . .
6   I like English food, although . . . .
7   Though I sometimes have dinner in a restaurant, ...
8   However good the wine may be, ...
9   Whatever some people may say of English food, ...
10   He gave me a big helping, although . . . .

E   Mark the strong (i.e. stressed) syllable in each word.

arrangement, canteen, vegetable, restaurant, residential,
practically, customers, waitresses, themselves, advantage

F   Write an account of a family dinner on a special occasion.

The big stores

One of the features of London is the number of big stores, most of which are to be found in or near the West End. They are vast buildings, many storeys high; in them you may buy almost anything you want, from a box of matches to a suite of furniture. Most of them are very modern and are equipped with speedy lifts and escalators, and have well-planned lighting, ventilation and heating. You can spend hours wandering around one of these stores, and you will probably lose your way while you are doing so, in spite of the notices pointing the way to the lifts and entrances. If you have been in the store so long that you feel hungry, you will not need to leave the building, for nearly all the big stores have cafés, snack bars or restaurants. You can ring up a friend from a telephone-box and you may call at the theatre agency to book a seat for an evening show; or you may drop into the travel department and arrange for a holiday in Wales or Western Australia. If you feel homesick, you will be able to get a newspaper or magazine from your own country at the newspaper counter; and in the book department you will be able to buy the complete works of William

The assistants will help you to choose.

Shakespeare or the latest thriller. You can inspect the goods on sale at your leisure, and you will not be pestered to buy, though occasionally an assistant may ask whether he can be of help to you.

Although shops usually close at 5.30 or 6 p.m., on Thursdays the West End stores and most other shops there stay open as late as eight o'clock. As it is early closing day in many London suburbs, a large number of people come into town on Thursdays for a special shopping afternoon. The Thursday evening rush-hour in the West End is probably the worst of the week.

Another feature of London's shopping life is the chain-store, in which prices are low and a wide variety of goods is offered—chiefly foodstuffs, household goods, clothing and stationery. The goods are displayed on open counters and it is a regrettable fact that some shop-lifting goes on, in spite of the vigilance of the store detectives. These chain-stores have branches in most British towns of importance. They keep their prices low, thanks to careful 'bulk-buying'. One very well known firm of chemists also has shops in many parts of London (and elsewhere); here you may buy not only medicines but also cosmetics and toilet supplies.

Many of the food stores now operate on the 'serve yourself' method: you go in, pick up a basket, walk round the shop and choose what you want. At the exit there is a cash-desk where you pay for all your goods together. This system cuts down the firm's expenses, for fewer assistants are required. It is the method used in the great and still growing number of London's supermarkets—large self-service stores chiefly concerned with the sale of foodstuffs but increasingly with other types of goods as well.

A   Vocabulary

1   What is meant by *feature* in 'A feature of London'?
2   Give the meanings of *story* and *storey*, and state their plurals.
3   Give the meanings of these expressions.
equipped with, a thriller, a suburb, ventilation, to pester
4   Give antonyms for *speedy*; *the exit*.
5   To what may the word *suite* refer, besides furniture?
Give a homophone for *suite*. (Homophones are words of different spellings, but with the same sound.)

6   Give the meaning of these phrases.
to book a seat, bulk buying, to feel homesick, early closing day,
to cut down
7   Give the nouns corresponding to the following.
speedy, to lose, to thrill, to display, to add, to ventilate, hungry,
wide, to choose, to subtract
8   Give the meanings of *stationary* and *stationery*; *diary* and *dairy*;
produce (noun) and *product*.

B   Questions on 'The big stores'

1   In what part of London are most of the big stores
situated?
2   What can you buy in the big stores?
3   Name three facilities offered by most of the big stores.
4   What is the attitude of the assistants about asking shoppers
what they want to buy?
5   Why do many people come to shop in the West End on
Thursdays?
6   What, unfortunately, makes shop-lifting easy in chain-stores?
7   Why are prices low in chain-stores?
8   Where do you pay for your goods in most food stores?
9   How do many chain-stores cut down the number of
assistants needed?
10   What is a 'supermarket'?

C   Grammar

1   Give the past simple and the past and present participles of
these verbs.
feel, plan, light, spend, ring, keep, lend, offer, equip, sell
2   Insert in each of the following sentences the missing relative
pronoun (who, etc.; which; that). If the pronoun may be
omitted, put it in brackets.
  a There are stores in . . . . you can buy almost anything
  under the sun.
  b The London stores are the biggest . . . . I have ever seen.

c There is nothing . . . . you cannot buy in such stores.

d The assistant, ... was very helpful, showed me many articles.

e The assistant, to . . . . I gave the article, wrapped it up very carefully.

f The saving . . . . is made in that way is very important.

g People . . . . time is limited often shop in big stores.

h The goods . . . . you want can all be bought at one shop.

i The staff, ... are well paid, have a canteen on the premises.

j The staff council, ... is composed of elected representatives, does much good work.

3 Complete the following sentences by inserting in the blank spaces *up, down, into, at, for, in, round, on, to* as needed.

a It takes hours to go . . . . a big store.

b I want you to call . . . . the dairy on your way home.

c I called . . . . Mr. Smith but he was not . . . . home.

d I heard somebody calling . . . . help.

e Friends are liable to drop . . . . at any hour of the day.

f Let's find a lift. I want to go . . . . the fifth floor.

g Look . . . . all the people round that car! I wonder what is going . . . .

h You pay . . . . your purchases . . . . the cash-desk . . . . the exit.

i You can change your books . . . . the nearest branch, which is just . . . . the corner.

j You should cut . . . . the number of cigarettes that you smoke every day.

D Write an essay on one of the following subjects.

1 Shopping in a big town
2 Shopping in a little village
3 Shopping for someone's birthday
4 Shopping for the holidays

A Police-court

Even a careful motorist may have the misfortune to commit a motoring offence. In due course, having received a summons, he ·will appear in what is commonly known as a police-court. This is a court presided over by a magistrate, who tries cases without a jury. A magistrate has powers to pass sentence for relatively minor offences only; serious charges are dealt with by a judge and jury. In certain cases, the accused may choose to go before a judge and jury, instead of appearing before a magistrate. A magistrate's court is also used for the conduct of preliminary enquiries to determine whether or not an accused person shall appear for trial in a higher court.

When his case comes up in court, the motorist hears his name called by the clerk of the court, and comes forward to identify

Outside London, courts are presided over by three magistrates. In this scene from a television film a solicitor is questioning a witness.

himself. The magistrate then calls for the policeman who charged the offender and asks him to give evidence. The officer takes the oath to 'tell the truth, the whole truth, and nothing but the truth.' He also is expected to give an account of what happened when the offence was committed and to mention any special circumstances. For instance, the offence may have been partly due to the foolishness of another motorist. It would be unwise for the accused motorist to exaggerate this. It will not help his case to try to blame someone else for his own mistake. The magistrate, on hearing that some other motorist is involved, will doubtless say: 'What is being done about this man?' 'Case coming up later this afternoon,' may well be the answer.

If you are guilty, it is of course wise to plead guilty and apologize for committing the offence and taking up the court's time. Magistrates are not heartless and a motorist may be lucky enough to hear one say: 'There are mitigating circumstances, but you have broken the law and I am obliged to impose a fine. Pay five pounds. Next case.' For many offences, if you wish to plead guilty you may do so by post and avoid attending the court at all.

Some short-tempered people forget that both policemen and magistrates have a public duty to perform, and are rude to them. This does not pay—and rightly so! A magistrate will not let off an offender merely because he is respectful, but the courteous lawbreaker may certainly hope that the magistrate will extend to him what tolerance the law permits.

A   Vocabulary

1   What sort of actions may one *commit*?
2   What, generally speaking, is the difference between an *offence* and a *crime*?
3   What is a *jury*?
4   What is an *oath*? Give the verb meaning *to take an oath* (with its past tense and present and past participles).
5   With what verb is *trial* connected?
6   Explain the following.
preliminary, a couple of, a summons, a witness, to blame, to plead guilty, to mitigate, a fine, to be let off lightly

7   Explain the sense of the phrasal verb given in italics in the following sentences.

   a I *called on* my friend yesterday.
   b He *called upon* me to help him.
   c I *called at* his house but he was out.
   d The match has been *called off*.
   e This exercise *calls for* a good sense of balance.

8   Explain what is meant by *account* in these sentences.

   a Your *account* of your journey is most interesting.
   b I have an *account* with the Bank of Scotland.
   c Can you *account* for the magistrate's behaviour?

9   For what kind of things may one apologize?

10 Give the nouns corresponding to the following.
guilty, innocent, firm, pay, courteous

11 What did the magistrate mean when he said 'Next case'?

B   Questions on 'A Police-court'

1   For what may even a prudent motorist receive a summons?
2   What is a police-court?
3   Who deals with serious charges?
4   What does a witness promise to tell?
5   What special circumstances might a policeman mention when giving evidence?
6   What attitude should a man take if he knows he is guilty?
7   What might make a magistrate deal leniently with an offender?
8   What attitude to policemen does not pay?
9   Is there any advantage in being polite in court?
10 What kind of people are sometimes rude to magistrates and policemen?

C   Grammar

1   Insert the verb (given in brackets) in the past simple or the past perfect, as needed in the following sentences.

   a I was worried when I . . . . (receive) a summons.

b I was more worried after I . . . . (see) my lawyer.

c I . . . . (stand) up when the clerk called out my name.

d When the policeman . . . . (take) the oath, he gave evidence.

e The magistrate fined me lightly after the policeman . . . . (speak) favourably of me.

f After I . . . . (finish) my work, I went out.

g I . . . . (go) out, ... (walk) some way and then . . . . (realize) that I . . . . (leave) my umbrella in the house.

h After we . . . . (see) the sights, we felt a little tired.

i When he . . . . (come) in, he smiled at me.

j By five o'clock I . . . . (finish) all my work.

2 Give the past tense and the past and present participles of these verbs.

commit, choose, hear, give, break, let, deal

3 Insert the missing prepositions in the following sentences.

a The court was presided . . . . by an elderly magistrate.

b The murderer was sentenced . . . . life imprisonment.

c He was found guilty . . . . stealing a purse.

d . . . . my surprise our team lost the match.

e A young solicitor spoke . . . . defence . . . . the accused man.

f Have you heard . . . . Tom recently? He hasn't written to me.

g Have you heard . . . . the latest cure for colds?

h The boy apologized . . . . me . . . . his rudeness.

i He imposed a fine . . . . the offender.

j That man will appear . . . . two days' time.

D Write an account of an accident (real or imaginary) that you have seen.

Buying books

Londoners are great readers. They buy vast numbers of newspapers and magazines and even of books—especially paperbacks, which are still comparatively cheap in spite of ever-increasing rises in the costs of printing. They still continue to buy 'proper' books, too, printed on good paper and bound between hard covers.

There are many streets in London containing shops which specialize in book-selling. Perhaps the best known of these is Charing Cross Road in the very heart of London. Here bookshops of all sorts and sizes are to be found, from the celebrated one which boasts of being 'the biggest bookshop in the world' to the tiny, dusty little places which seem to have been left over from Dickens' time. Some of these shops stock, or will obtain, any kind of book, but many of them specialize—in second-hand books, in art books, in foreign books, in books on philosophy, politics or any other of the myriad subjects about which books may be written. One shop in this area specializes solely in books about ballet!

Although it may be the most convenient place for Londoners to buy books, Charing Cross Road is not the cheapest. For the really

One of London's famous bookshops where you can browse or buy

cheap second-hand volumes, the collector must venture off the beaten track, to Farringdon Road, for example, in the East Central district of London. Here there is nothing so grandiose as bookshops. Instead, the booksellers come along each morning and tip out their sacks of books on to small barrows which line the gutters. And the collectors, some professional and some amateur, who have been waiting for them, pounce upon the dusty cascade. In places like this one can still, occasionally, pick up for a few pence an old volume that may be worth many pounds.

Both Charing Cross Road and Farringdon Road are well-known haunts of the book buyer. Yet all over London there are bookshops, in places not so well known, where the wares are equally varied and exciting. It is in the sympathetic atmosphere of such shops that the ardent book buyer feels most at home. In these shops, even the life-long book-browser is frequently rewarded by the accidental discovery of previously unknown delights. One could, in fact, easily spend a lifetime exploring London's bookshops. There are many less pleasant ways of spending time!

Hunting for book bargains

A   Vocabulary

1   What is the difference between a *magazine* and a *book*?
2   Find a synonym for *cheap*.
3   What is the difference between a *paperback* and an ordinary book?
4   What is the meaning of *grandiose*?
5   *Stock* may be either verb or noun. What does it mean in each case?
6   Find an alternative for *myriad*.
7   What is a *track*?
8   Explain the meaning of *to venture off the beaten track*.
9   What is a *barrow*?
10   What part of the street is the *gutter*?
11   Find a synonym for *cascade*.
12   What verb is *to pick up* the colloquial equivalent of?
13   What is a *haunt*?
14   A *book-browser* is someone who browses among books. What does *to browse* mean?
15   What are *wares*? Is this word normally used in the singular?

B   Questions on 'Buying books'

1   What type of reading do Londoners seem to indulge in most of all?
2   What is the main advantage of 'paperbacks' compared with 'hardbacks'?
3   Which is the best known book-selling district in London?
4   How are books sold in Farringdon Road?
5   What is the difference between Charing Cross Road and Farringdon Road from the book buyer's point of view?
6   Why does the ardent book buyer feel most at home in some of the smaller bookshops?
7   With what is he frequently rewarded in the smaller bookshops?
8   How long do you think it could take to explore all London's bookshops?
9   Are there bookshops in other parts of London?

C Grammar

1 Put the following sentences into the passive.
   a We had finished all the work by nine o'clock.
   b I shall pay all my bills tomorrow.
   c The rescue party found the missing climber after a long search.
   d We were making good progress until the car broke down.
   e I did a little work but my friend did a great deal.
   f I will forgive you because you are sorry.
2 Put the verbs in the following sentences into the future tense, the present tense or the imperative.
   a If you have planted them correctly, the flowers . . . . (bloom).
   b If it rains, we . . . . (not, go out) this afternoon.
   c You . . . . (feel) better if you . . . . (drink) your medicine.
   d He . . . . (return) shortly unless he has had trouble with the car.
   e If there . . . . (be) no answer when you . . . . (knock) at the door . . . . (enter) without waiting.
   f It will snow if the temperature . . . . (fall) any more.

D Make up sentences using the following verbs so as to bring out their meaning as fully as possible.

to overlook, to undergo, to overcome, to undertake, to overturn, to underrate, to overtake, to underline, to overrun, to undercut

E Write an essay on 'My favourite author'.

Going to the theatre

London is very rich in theatres; there are over forty in the West End alone—more than enough to ensure that there will always be at least two or three shows running to suit every kind of taste, whether serious or frivolous.

Some of them are specialist theatres. The Royal Opera House, Covent Garden, where the great opera singers of the world can be heard, is the home of opera and The Royal Ballet. The London Coliseum now houses the English National Opera Company, which encourages English singers in particular and performs most operas in English at popular prices.

Some theatres concentrate on the classics and serious drama, some on light comedy and revue, some on musicals. Most theatres have a personality of their own, from the old, such as the Theatre Royal (the 'Haymarket') in the Haymarket, to the more modern such as the recently opened Barbican centre in the City. The National Theatre has three separate theatres in its new building by Waterloo Bridge. At the new Barbican centre the Royal Shakespeare

An old fashioned theatre. The City Varieties Theatre, Leeds.

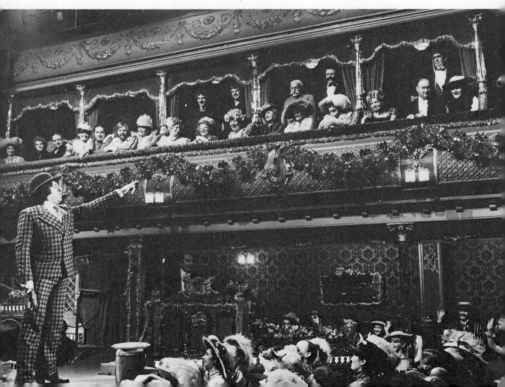

Company have their London home—their other theatre is at Stratford-on-Avon.

Most of the older London theatres are concentrated in a very small area, within a stone's throw of the Piccadilly and Leicester Square tube stations. As the evening performances normally begin either at seven-thirty or eight p.m. there is a kind of minor rush-hour between seven-fifteen and eight o'clock in this district. People stream out of the nearby tube stations, the pavements are crowded, and taxis and private cars manoeuvre into position as they drop theatre-goers outside the entrance to each theatre. There is another minor rush-hour when the performance finishes. The theatre in London is very popular and it is not always easy to get in to see a successful play.

Before World War II theatre performances began later and a visit to the theatre was a more formal occasion. Nowadays very few people 'dress' for the theatre (that is, wear formal evening dress)

The National Theatre – a modern approach to theatre design

except for first nights or an important 'gala' performance. The times of performance were put forward during the war and have not been put back. The existing times make the question of eating a rather tricky problem: one has to have either early dinner or late supper. Many restaurants in 'theatreland' ease the situation by catering specially for early or late diners.

Television and the difficulty of financing plays have helped to close many theatres. But it seems that the worst of the situation is now over and that the theatre, after a period of decline, is about to pick up again. Although some quite large provincial towns do not have a professional theatre, there are others, such as Nottingham, Hull, Coventry or Newcastle, which have excellent repertory companies and where a series of plays are performed during one season by a resident group of actors. Some towns such as Chichester or Edinburgh have theatres which give summer seasons. Even in small towns a number of theatres have been built in the last few years to cater for the local population.

A   Vocabulary

1   Explain, or give equivalents for, the following phrases.
'there are many shows *running* at the present time', 'within *a
stone's throw* of Piccadilly', 'people *stream out* of the nearby tube
stations', 'a rather *tricky* problem', 'the theatre is about to *pick up*
again'
2   *a* What is the collective noun for the people who watch
       a play?
    b What is a *revue*?
    c What are the *classics*?
    d What is a *musical*?

B   Questions on 'Going to the theatre'

1   How many theatres are there in the West End of London?
2   What would you see on a visit to Covent Garden?
3   What is special about the National Theatre?
4   Where would you find many of London's theatres?
5   What would you notice about the streets in this area
between seven fifteen and eight p.m.?
6   What difference did the war make to theatre-going?
7   What two things have had a bad effect on the theatre in
England?
8   What is the present situation in the theatre?

C   Grammar

1   Put the verbs in the following sentences into the simple
or continuous present.
    a He .... to the theatre twice a week. (go)
    b That actor always .... a good performance. (give)
    c The curtain .... at seven thirty every evening. (rise)
    d I think we .... in the wrong seats. (sit)
    e When 'God Save the Queen' is played everyone ....
    (stand up)
    f I often .... to opera on gramophone records. (listen)

g Which actor .... the main part? (take)

h I do not think the heroine .... very well tonight. (perform)

2   Give the past tense, past participle and present participle of these verbs.

ensure, begin, jostle, come, know, see, finance, think, do

3   Give the nouns corresponding to the following adjectives.

formal, entertaining, special, tricky, relative, young, feeble, high, rewarding

D   Complete the following sentences.

1   The theatre was so full that ....
2   The traffic was so dense we ....
3   The hero was good but ....
4   I like old theatres best because ....
5   There is always one show in London that ....
6   When the curtain rose we saw ....
7   Because the play was boring I ....
8   I should prefer the theatre to start later as ....
9   Never arrive late at the theatre because ....
10   The tenor was ill and therefore ....

E   Mark the strong stresses in the following words.

concentrated, entertainment, theatre, ballet, performance, recently, relative, decline, professional

F   Write an essay on any play you have enjoyed seeing or reading.

'Pubs'

Owing to the uncertainty of the weather, outdoor cafés are not a feature of English life. Their place is partly filled by what are colloquially known as 'pubs', public houses. Here you can get any form of alcoholic drink, from beer to whisky, or—nowadays— soft drinks. Many pubs also run some kind of snack bar that provides cold food such as sausages, ham, olives, salad, veal-and-ham pie, rolls and butter and sometimes hot pies or toasted sandwiches.

Some pubs maintain the traditional division into two parts—a public bar and a saloon bar. In the first there is often a dart board, and groups of friends will gather in the pub for a friendly match. The loser may have to pay for a round! In the saloon bar your drinks cost a little more, but the atmosphere is quieter and there are perhaps fewer people. In many pubs there is also a restaurant,

A country pub with its thatched roof

Outside a popular London pub

and the food here is usually plain but of good quality; in fact, to taste good, traditional English food you would do well to visit a reputable pub. Many business men habitually have lunch in a pub near their office. In the country, the pub is often part of an inn where you can put up for the night.

The Englishman's favourite drink is beer, of which a variety of sorts is brewed; 'bitter' is probably the most popular. 'Stout' is a heavy dark beer, very popular in Ireland. English beer is different from Continental beer; the latter should be served well chilled, whereas English beer is at its best when it is only cool. Continental-type beer or 'lager' has become very popular in England in recent years and its sales are beginning to rival those of the more traditional beers. Wine is also increasingly drunk, both in pubs and in the home.

The times of opening of pubs are regulated by law; local variations are possible but usually a pub is open from half past eleven to three o'clock and from half past five to half past ten or eleven o'clock. Betting is forbidden in pubs and children are not allowed on licensed premises. In the old days, when people drank too much and pubs were often rowdy, the law against children entering pubs was a wise one. Today, however, increasing numbers of pubs are opening their gardens to customers, so that children can play safely while their parents have a quiet drink.

It would be quite wrong to consider the average English pub as anything other than a respectable, friendly place that provides good drink, good food and a pleasant social atmosphere. Far too often the foreigner has read accounts of sordid nineteenth-century drinking places, haunted by people whose one desire was to drink as much as they could afford as quickly as possible.

Another fairly widespread idea is that people do not sit down in English pubs, whereas they often do. This misconception probably arises from the origin of the word 'bar', which referred to the metal rod (bar) along the lower edge of the counter, where the customer could rest his foot while standing up to have his drink. English pubs do not resemble the 'saloons' shown in the more fanciful Wild West films!

A   Vocabulary

1   Explain what is meant by these phrases.
a feature, colloquial, reputable, to haunt, a soft drink, a misconception, a dart, whereas, to brew, fanciful, a counter, an inn, stout (adjective), to regulate, sordid
On what syllable is the adjective *frequent* stressed? And the verb *to frequent*?

2   Express the following phrases in other words.
to pay for a round, you would do well to, to put up at an inn, to put up with someone, licensed premises

3   Express in other words the meaning of the words in *italics* in the following sentences.
  a They *run a snack bar*.
  b I *ran into* Smith yesterday.
  c Jim's in hospital: he was *run over* by a car.
  d You should not *run up* bills.
  e Please *run through* what I have written.
  f The milk boiled and *ran over* onto the stove.

B   Questions on 'Pubs'

1   Why are there few outdoor cafés in England?
2   What is a pub?
3   What is the difference between the public bar and the saloon bar?
4   What sort of food does one usually get in a pub?
5   State one way in which English beer is different from Continental beer.
6   Why is it not possible to get into a pub at certain times of the day?
7   Describe several ways in which pubs have changed since the old days.
8   Describe the atmosphere in an average English public house.
9   Why is it that some foreigners have wrong ideas about English pubs?
10 What is the origin of the word *bar*?

C   Grammar

1   Give the past simple and the past and present participles of these verbs.
forbid, bet, rise, raise, arise

2   Insert the correct form of *rise, raise* or *arise* in the following
sentences.

    a You should have . . . . your hat to that lady.
    b If trouble . . . . over it, be particularly prudent.
    c The aeroplane . . . . swiftly. (Use the past simple.)
    d We watched the tide . . . .
    e They have at last . . . . my salary.
    f No fresh difficulties have . . . .
    g . . . . your hand if you know the answer.
    h The sun . . . . at half past seven yesterday.
    i He . . . . to be President of his country.
    j Since that time prices have . . . . considerably.

3   Give the adjectives corresponding to the following words.
nature, obtain, pay, pity, atmosphere, desire, tradition, friend,
commerce, taste

D   Write an essay on one of the following subjects.

1   An outdoor café in your own country
2   An old inn that you know
3   What you expect of a good hotel

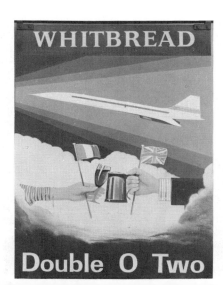

Public holidays

In England, Christmas Day and Good Friday have been holidays (literally 'Holy Days') for religious reasons since the establishment of Christianity in this country. Christmas is celebrated on December 25, not Christmas Eve as in several other European countries. The other public holidays (or 'Bank Holidays') are Easter Monday, May Day (May 1st), the Spring Bank Holiday (the last Monday in May), the Summer Bank Holiday (the last Monday in August), December 26th (Boxing Day), and New Year's Day. The term 'Bank Holiday' goes back to the Bank Holidays Act of 1871, which owes its name to the fact that banks are closed on the days specified.

Boxing Day takes its name from the old custom of giving employees or tradesmen (such as the milkman) an annual present or 'Christmas box' on that day. It has nothing to do with the sport of 'boxing'! If Christmas Day or Boxing Day falls at the weekend, the

A funfair at Stratford-upon-Avon.

weekday which follows December 25th and 26th becomes a Bank Holiday.

Easter Monday is generally regarded as an unofficial consecration of Spring. In many towns there are funfairs with roundabouts, coconut-shies, switchbacks and other amusements. The fair on Hampstead Heath, in the north of London, is particularly famous. Easter Monday used to be the day on which the ladies would parade in the parks, wearing new dresses and hats. Although this custom is dying out, the tradition still provides the ladies with a pretext for buying spring clothes.

The August Bank Holiday is probably the most popular one of the year, partly because it comes at a time when children are not at school. Very many people try to make this a long week-end, and go away to the seaside or the country (as they may indeed have done at Easter or in Spring). The result is that anyone who can manage to take a holiday at another time would be well advised to do so, for the roads get congested with traffic (in England, at the time of writing, there are more vehicles per mile of road than in any other country).

A traffic 'jam'

In recent years, there has been a good deal of talk of creating another Bank Holiday mid-way between August and Christmas, but nothing has yet been done. October would be a good month, as the weather is often very agreeable then. Many people would welcome an extra 'Bank Holiday' or two as England has fewer than most Continental countries.

In Ireland, St Patrick's Day (March 17th) is also a Bank Holiday. St Patrick is the Patron Saint of Ireland. It is curious that St George's Day (April 23rd) is not a public holiday in England, for St George is the Patron Saint of England, and in addition that day is the anniversary of the birth of the most famous of Englishmen, William Shakespeare. However, the flag of St George (a red cross on a white background) or the Union Jack is flown on that day, particularly by churches of the Church of England.

The public holidays in Scotland are New Year's Day and the second of January (the third, if the first or second of January is a Sunday), Good Friday, May Day and usually the first Monday in August. There are local variations. New Year's Eve is called Hogmanay in Scotland and is an occasion for much joyous and noisy celebration. It is a Scottish tradition that the first person to cross the threshold of your house on New Year's Day should be dark-haired—such a person brings luck for the coming year. In London, Scottish people gather on the steps of St Paul's Cathedral and sing 'Auld Lang Syne' at midnight. There are also large crowds in Piccadilly Circus and Trafalgar Square, and New Year's Eve is a great occasion for parties and jollity.

A   Vocabulary

1   Give the meaning of these phrases.
the Union Jack, congested, to celebrate, the threshold, a tradesman, jollity, a pretext, to parade, to create, joyous, a great occasion

2   What is meant by *act* (as in Bank Holidays Act)? What is meant by *specified* (as in 'banks are closed on the days specified')?

3   Explain what you do on a *roundabout,* at a *coconut-shy,* on a *switchback.*

4   Explain what is meant by *fair* or *fairly* in the following
sentences.

　　a Sheila has fair hair.
　　b It isn't fair! Your share is bigger than mine.
　　c The children enjoyed the fair in the village.
　　d We admired the machines we saw at the British Industries
　　Fair.
　　e Don't cheat! You should play fair.
　　f There was a fair amount of applause.
　　g He was fairly tired when he arrived.
　　h I like sailing when the weather is fair.

5   Write a sentence using *occasion* and one using *occasionally*.

B   Questions on 'Public holidays'

1   What is the name given to public holidays in Britain?
2   What is the origin of the term 'Boxing Day'?
3   What used to be special about Easter Monday for women?
4   Why is the Late Summer Bank Holiday so popular?
5   What do many people do for August Bank Holiday?
6   What are the roads like on August Bank Holiday?
7   What new holiday might be created?
8   With what is April 23rd connected?
9   What is the Scottish tradition concerning New Year's Day?
10 Is New Year's Eve passed over in silence in England?

C   Grammar

1   Insert the verb (given in brackets) in a correct form in each
of the following sentences.

　　a The Government said that from that year certain days
　　.... (be) public holidays.
　　b Christmas Day has had special significance ever since
　　Christianity .... (come) to England.
　　c I have learnt something about English public holidays
　　since I .... (be) in England.
　　d In those days postmen .... (receive) Christmas boxes.

e This custom . . . . (die) out but has not quite disappeared.
f When the roads are full of traffic, some foolish motorists
. . . . (get) over-impatient.
g They have only made plans, they . . . . (not do) anything
yet.
h While Tom . . . . (ride) on the switchback, his hat blew off.
i After you . . . . (celebrate) New Year's Eve, you may feel a
little tired.
j Tell me what you . . . . (see) at the village fair this afternoon.

2   Put the adverbs (given in brackets) in a correct place in each
of the following sentences.

a Tom leaves for the office at eight o'clock. (generally)
b I cannot tell you but this is what I know about it.
(officially)
c It was stated that Monday was to be a holiday. (officially)
d That serious-looking man is a teacher. (probably)
e You should examine the matter. (carefully)
f He is growing fatter and fatter. (steadily)
g The fair is held just outside the village. (usually)
h On entering the church, he took off his hat. (naturally)
i I wish you would speak your words. At present you
sound most affected! (naturally)
j They celebrated New Year's Eve, with music and laughter.
(gaily)

D   Write an essay on your National Holiday or (if you have
been in Britain) on a British Bank Holiday.

The British Bobby

The English policeman has several nicknames but the most frequently used are 'copper' and 'bobby'. The first name comes from the verb to 'cop' (which is also slang), meaning to 'take' or 'capture', and the second comes from the first name of Sir Robert Peel, the nineteenth century politician, who was the founder of the police force as we know it to-day. An early nickname for the policeman was 'peeler', but this one has died out.

Whatever we may call them, the general opinion of the police seems to be a favourable one; except, of course, among the criminal part of the community where the police are given more derogatory nicknames which originated in America, such as 'fuzz' or 'pig'. Visitors to England seem, nearly always, to be very impressed by the English police. It has, in fact, become a standing joke that the visitor to Britain, when asked for his views of the country, will always say, at some point or other, 'I think your policemen are wonderful.'

Well, the British bobby may not always be wonderful but he is usually a very friendly and helpful sort of character. A music-hall song of some years ago was called, 'If You Want To Know The Time Ask A Policeman'. Nowadays, most people own watches but they

The police have plenty of experience in crowd control.

still seem to find plenty of other questions to ask the policeman. In London, the policemen spend so much of their time directing visitors about the city that one wonders how they ever find time to do anything else!

Two things are immediately noticeable to the stranger, when he sees an English policeman for the first time. The first is that he does not carry a pistol and the second is that he wears a very distinctive type of headgear, the policeman's helmet. His helmet, together with his height, enables an English policeman to be seen from a considerable distance, a fact that is not without its usefulness. From time to time it is suggested that the policeman should be given a pistol and that his helmet should be taken from him, but both these suggestions are resisted by the majority of the public and the police themselves. However, the police have not resisted all changes: radios, police-cars and even helicopters give them greater mobility now.

The policeman's lot is not an enviable one, even in a country which prides itself on being reasonably law-abiding. But, on the whole, the English policeman fulfils his often thankless task with courtesy and good humour, and an understanding of the fundamental fact that the police are the country's servants and not its masters.

A   Vocabulary

1   What is a *nickname*?
2   What does one do if one *founds* something?
3   What is meant by *derogatory*?
4   The word *criminal* in the passage is an adjective. Can you give two nouns derived from this word?
5   What is a *standing* joke?
6   Find a word or phrase meaning the same as *nowadays*.
7   What do you do when you *direct* somebody?
8   What adjective can be derived from *mobility*?
9   Find a more common, simpler synonym for *headgear*.
10   What is the verb from the adjective *enviable*? What does it mean?
11   Find a synonym for *task*.

B   Questions on 'The British Bobby'

1   Who was Sir Robert Peel?
2   What is the general opinion of the English police?
3   Which people disagree with it?
4   What comment is always expected, sooner or later, from a visitor to Britain?
5   Why is it no longer necessary for most people to ask a policeman, if they wish to know the time?
6   What do policemen in London spend a large part of their time in doing?
7   What two things does a stranger immediately notice about an English policeman?
8   Why can an English policeman be seen from some distance away?
9   Why is it a good thing that a policeman can be seen from a distance?
10   What fundamental fact is the English policeman aware of?

C   Grammar

1   Use the correct form of the past simple or past continuous.
    a He . . . . (stop) when the policeman told him to.
    b As the convict . . . . (escape), he was seen by a warder.
    c The policeman . . . . (walk) along his beat when he was suddenly attacked.
    d He . . . . (start) when he heard a sudden noise.
    e He was caught by the police officer as he . . . . (break into) the shop.
    f The car . . . . (come up) to within a few inches of the policeman who was directing the traffic, and then stopped.
    g The witness . . . . (speak) very clearly when the judge questioned him.
    h As he jumped out of the car he . . . . (bump) his head on the roof.
2   Insert *rather* or *fairly* as needed in the following sentences.
    a I am . . . . pleased with the result, but it's not as good as expected.

b She looks . . . . charming in her new dress, doesn't she?
c I think I shall lie down; I am . . . . tired.
d He owns . . . . more than two thousand acres of land.
e I don't like Ronald; he is . . . . too sure of himself.
f I am . . . . sure of what to do, but I am not certain.

D   Put the following idiomatic expressions into a sentence.

to take care of, to put up with, to turn up, to make off,
to keep up, to break down, to cheer up, to put upon

E   Write an essay describing an experience (real or imaginary)
involving the police.

Howzzat!

The British have always been a nation of sport lovers and interest in all types of sport is as great today as it has ever been. Many sports which nowadays are played all over the world grew up to their present-day form in Britain. Football is perhaps the best example, but among the others are horse-racing, golf, lawn tennis and rowing.

Many people, both foreigners and British, consider cricket to be the most typically English of sports. It is true that cricket, unlike football, has until recently remained a specifically British game, played only in Britain, in some parts of the British Commonwealth and in Denmark. But it would be wrong to say that cricket is the most *popular* British sport: that is, undoubtedly, football. Nevertheless, it remains true that for most Englishmen the sight of white-flannelled cricketers on the smooth green turf of a cricket pitch represents something that is traditionally English.

Cricket and football, however, are merely the two most popular sports in Britain: there are many others. In the summer, lawn tennis probably comes next in importance to cricket. There are clubs in every town and in all the parks there are public courts where tennis may be played for an hour on payment of about one pound. Swimming is very popular and there are many public swimming baths. Rowing and canoeing are practised less because there are not so many facilities. The annual Boat Race between Oxford and Cambridge universities on the river Thames is, however, one of the most popular sporting events of the year. Golf is becoming increasingly popular and many clubs are having

Left 'Tic-tac men' send strange signals about bets.
Right Racing at Goodwood

to turn prospective members away. Athletics is growing all the time.

The most popular winter sport, after football (or 'soccer' as it is colloquially called) is rugby football (or 'rugger') which remains a largely amateur game. Winter sports such as skiing are generally impossible in Britain (except in Scotland) owing to the unsuitable climate, but more and more people spend winter holidays on the Continent in order to take part in them.

One reason for the great interest in sport in Britain is the Englishman's fondness for a little 'flutter' (a slang expression for a bet or gamble). Gambling has always been an integral part of such sports as horse-racing and dog-racing and, in recent times, doing the 'football pools' has become a national pastime. But whether as gambler, spectator or player, most Englishmen have some interest in at least some sports.

Centre Court at Wimbledon Tennis Tournament.

A   Vocabulary

1   Name three sports not mentioned in the passage.
2   Distinguish between *game* and *sport*.
3   Give another word for *integral* as in the expression
'an integral part'.
4   What are *white flannels*?
5   Tennis is played on a tennis *court*. Can you give the names
of two very different sorts of court?
6   Football is played on a football . . . . . Races are run on a
racing . . . . .
7   Give a synonym for *turn away* in the phrase 'to turn
prospective members away'.
8   What is the opposite of *amateur*? Explain the difference
between the two terms.
9   What is a *prospective* member?

B   Questions on 'Sport'

1   Which sports have originated, in their present form, in
Britain?
2   Which sport is regarded as typically English?
3   Which is the most popular British sport?
4   Why do many of the British take winter holidays on the
Continent?
5   Give one reason why many of the British are interested in
horse-racing.
6   What is the annual sporting event which takes place on the
river Thames?
7   Can you think of any reason for the popularity of this
event?

C   Grammar

1   Give the past tense, and past and present participles of these
verbs.
prevail, play, grow, oppose, leave, find, take

2   Make the following sentences negative, using *no* and *not
any*.
    a I have some cricket flannels.
    b They need some more practice. (N.B. *practice* is the noun
    form, *practise* the verb; the words are homophones.)
    c I scored some goals in the match.
    d I saw someone dive into the pool.
    e They lost some balls playing tennis.
    f We need more players like you.
3   Insert the correct prepositions in the following sentences.
    a He ran up . . . . the goal.
    b The player jumped . . . . the air to reach the ball.
    c The canoeist sat . . . . his canoe very confidently.
    d The boxer's fist flashed . . . . the air.
    e Always keep your eye . . . . the ball.
    f The diver suddenly sprang . . . . the top board.

D   Mark the strong syllable in each of the following words.

foreigners, specifically, popular, facilities, traditional, amateur,
integral, spectator

E   The large part sport has always played in English social life
may be seen from the considerable number of idiomatic
expressions derived from the various games. Can you give the
meaning of the following ten common expressions?

to play the game, to throw up the sponge, it isn't cricket,
to do something off one's own bat, to knock someone (or
something) for six, to be out for the count, to hit below the belt,
to be an outsider, to be left at the post, to be on the last lap

F   Write an essay on one or more sports which you enjoy
watching or playing.

T.V.

Television (colloquially known as 'T.V.' or 'the telly') is nowadays so popular in Britain that it is hard to believe that the first acceptable televised pictures were transmitted less than forty years ago. A pioneer team working at Hayes, Middlesex, were the first to produce what is known as 'high definition television', which gives pictures of moving objects clear enough to be enjoyed as entertainment.

The BBC was the first authority in the world to provide a public television service, which began in 1936. During the war transmissions ceased, but were resumed in 1946. Viewers are now able to watch television for many hours a day, if they have time and inclination. Moreover, viewers now have four channels at their disposal. In 1955 the Independent Broadcasting Authority opened a television service and in 1982 a second independent service came into operation. The BBC provides two channels. The viewing hours have also been extended with the introduction of breakfast television by both the BBC and the Independent Broadcasting Authority. Advertisers buy time for advertising on Independent Television, but the amount of time devoted to advertising is small; it is strictly limited by the special Act that allowed commercial television. Viewers of any of the programmes can watch plays, 'live' transmissions of topical events, sports and athletics, news features, interviews with prominent people, musical performances and many other items. Films are often televised, and many of them are made specially for television. The cinema industry is jealous of television, and understandably keeps new films for showing in cinemas; nevertheless, T.V. occasionally screens a premiere. Television has attracted many people away from the cinema and, in recent years, many cinemas have had to close. A frequent criticism of T.V. programmes is that they too often feature violence and gun-play. On the other hand, it must be said that religious programmes also are transmitted, and many serious and instructive matters are presented.

About ninety-five per cent of the population now have television in their homes. In 1982 there were over 18 million licences in force, and the revenue from these goes to the financing of the BBC transmissions. It is possible for many people to have TV sets, for although these are not cheap, there are ample facilities for renting sets or for hire-purchase.

Most programmes, whether BBC or ITV, are now transmitted

Top A televised discussion of a news item
Bottom A lot goes on behind the scenes.

in colour—but can of course also be received in black-and-white. The number of colour sets in use is very large. British television is linked with Europe through the Eurovision network. There is, however, no truth in the rumour that the experts have invented a method of broadcasting smells!

A   Vocabulary

1   What is the meaning of *colloquial, pioneer, item, hire-purchase, rumour, revenue*?

2   Give two sentences using the word *team*. Refer in one to animals, in the other to men.

3   Name a number of *entertainments*.

4   What is the meaning of *to cease*? What is the difference in pronunciation between *cease* and *seize*?

5   What does the abbreviation *BBC* stand for?

6   What do we call a person who watches television? And one who listens to sound radio?

7   Give a phrase of similar meaning to *at their disposal*.

8   Give a synonym for *strict* in the sentence 'He is a strict disciplinarian'.

9   What is the difference between *a play* and *a game*?

10   What is meant by *live* in 'a live transmission'? Give a word that rhymes with *live* used in this sense.

11   What is meant by *prominent people*?

12   Give words similar in meaning to *jealous, cheap, ample, to link*.

13   For what may we need a *licence*? (Name three things.)

14   Give a word opposite in meaning to *attract*.

15   Insert, as needed, the words *smell, scent, perfume, aroma, stink* in the following sentences.

  a These flowers have a delicate . . . .
  b I don't like the . . . . of disinfectant.
  c A pleasant . . . . of freshly-made coffee pervaded the flat.
  d The customs officer asked if I had bought any . . . . in Paris.
  e What a . . . . ! That egg must be six months old!

B   Questions on 'T.V.'

1   How long ago were the first good television pictures broadcast?

2   Who produced the first television able to give entertainment?

3   When did the first public television service start?

4   Why did transmissions cease in 1939?

5   Why is the amount of time devoted to advertising comparatively small?
6   What sort of things can one watch on television?
7   Why is the cinema industry jealous of television?
8   For what is T.V. sometimes blamed?
9   How do many people acquire their T.V. sets?
10   Is it likely that smells will soon be broadcast?

C   Grammar

1   Using a *prefix,* give opposites for these words.
popular, acceptable, clear, limited, understand
2   What is the difference in usage between *live* and *alive*?
3   Give the past tense and the past and present participles of these verbs.
transmit, broadcast, cease, seize, limit
4   Complete the following sentences.
   a Dancing is now more popular . . . . it was . . . .
   b The theatre is not . . . . popular . . . . it was . . . .
   c Football is . . . . popular sport of all in Britain.
   d This old actor is . . . . popular . . . . he was when . . . .
   e He is not . . . . foolish . . . . he . . . .
5   In the following sentences put the verb (given in brackets) in the correct form of the present tense (singular or plural) and select, where necessary, the right possessive adjective.
   a Our team . . . . (be) discussing its/their chances of success.
   b The audience . . . . (be) the largest we have ever had.
   c The herd . . . . (represent) much capital expenditure for the farmer.
   d The congregation . . . . (kneel) to say its/their prayers.
   e The Government . . . . (be) composed of clever fools!

D   Write an essay on 'The Influence of Radio' or 'The Influence of Television'.

Football pools

The English have never shown themselves averse to a gamble, though fortunately most of them know where to draw the line, and wisely refrain from betting excessively. Since the war the most widespread form of mild gambling is no doubt that of staking a small sum on the Football Pools. (The word 'pool' is connected with the picture of streams of money pouring into a common fund, or 'pool' from which the winners are paid after the firm has deducted its expenses and profit.) Those who do so receive every week from one of the pools firms a printed form; on this are listed the week's matches. Against each match, or against a number of them, the optimist puts down a 1, a 2 or an x to show that he thinks the result of the match will be a home win, an away win or a draw, respectively. The form is then posted to the pools firm, with a postal order or cheque for the amount staked (or, as the firms say, 'invested'). At the end of the week the results of the matches are announced on television and published in the newspapers and the 'investor' can take out his copy of his coupon and check his forecast.

If one sent in a correct forecast, one might win a fortune, for some of the rewards for guessing accurately eight drawn matches have been of over half a million pounds. Naturally, this does not happen every week. However, no doubt a man would still consider himself lucky if he won twenty thousand pounds.

A form or 'coupon' for the football pools

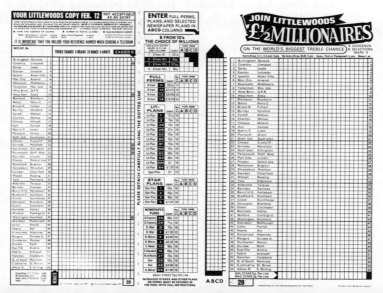

Anyone lucky enough to win a really large sum would be able to retire, or perhaps set up a little business of his own. The pools firms recognise a responsibility towards the winners of large sums and employ experts to give winners advice, if they wish it, on how best to invest their newly-acquired wealth. Not all of them take such advice, but the majority do. Most of the big pools wins have gone to people who are not very well-off and generally they have used the money wisely, buying themselves a house and a car, adding some luxuries to their daily life, but not throwing the money away on riotous living. Very many winners have at once spent part of their fortune on helping less fortunate relatives.

A win on the pools is as unexpected as a punch on the jaw!

A Vocabulary

1 Give an expression opposite in meaning to *averse to*.

2 Give a word of similar meaning to *fortunately*, in 'Fortunately they know when to stop'.

3 What is the meaning of *widespread*?

4 What is a *stake*? Give two meanings.

5 What is the sense of *against* in 'Against each match we put a mark'?

6 What is the opposite of an *optimist*?

7 Give another word for *pool* in 'There are some fish in that pool'.

8 What is a *postal order*?

9 In what does one usually *invest*?

10 What does *to guess* mean?

11 Give an opposite for *reward* in 'We are rewarded for good actions and . . . . for bad deeds'.

12 Find a synonym for *happen* in 'Something strange happened yesterday'.

13 Replace the expression *no doubt* by one word (of similar meaning) in 'The letter will no doubt arrive soon'.

14 What is an *expert*? Can the word be used as an adjective?

15 Give the verb corresponding to the noun *advise*.

16 What is meant by 'well-off'?

B Questions on 'Football pools'

1 Do the English like gambling?

2 Do they generally go too far when gambling?

3 What do investors in the pools have to forecast?

4 How can they check whether their results are correct?

5 Can one win a lot of money from the pools?

6 What sort of people have often won big prizes?

7 How do the pools firms help winners of big sums?

8 What is the behaviour of most winners of fortunes?

9 Whom do many winners help?

10 Is *all* the money invested in the pools shared out among the winners?

C Grammar

1 Give the past tense and the past and present participles of these verbs.

cast, send, win, buy, throw, pay

2 Insert the missing preposition or adverb.

a Here is a reward . . . . your bravery.
b I want to set . . . . a business of my own.
c These streams all run . . . . that lake.
d Please pour . . . . a cup of tea for Aunt Jane.
e Invest your money . . . . a reputable firm.
f Please add that . . . . my bill.
g I am not averse . . . . apple-juice.
h Always refrain . . . . excess of any sort.
i . . . . the end of the week you will know the result.
j He made a fortune of . . . . a million pounds.

3 Insert the verbs (given in brackets) in the correct tense in the following sentences.

a I should jump for joy if I . . . . (win) a big prize.
b What . . . . (you, do) if there was an accident?
c I . . . . (ask) a policeman the way if I were lost.
d I . . . . (help) my poorer relatives if I became rich.
e Would you ring up the doctor if you . . . . (feel) ill?
f If you . . . . (be) in doubt, would you consult a dictionary?
g Would you still go there tomorrow if it . . . . (rain) then?
h We should go to a better hotel if we . . . . (have) more money.
i Life would be easier if we . . . . (be) kinder to one another.
j Would you be frightened if you . . . . (meet) a tiger?

4 Using prefixes, form the opposites of these words.

fortunate, wise, correct, accurate, natural, moral, responsible, employed, prudent, lucky

D Write an essay on 'The Evils of Gambling'.

The peoples of Britain

Many foreigners who have not visited Britain call all the inhabitants 'English', for they are used to thinking of the British Isles as 'England'. In fact, the British Isles contain a variety of peoples and only the people of England call themselves English. The others refer to themselves as Welsh, Scottish, or Irish, as the case may be; they are often slightly annoyed at being classified as 'English'.

Even in England there are many differences in regional character and speech. The chief division is between southern England and northern England. South of a line going from Bristol to London, people speak the type of English usually learnt by foreign students, though there are local variations.

Further north (roughly beyond a line going from Manchester to Hull) regional speech is usually 'broader' than that of southern Britain. Northerners are apt to claim that they work harder than the Southerners, and are more thorough. They are open-hearted and hospitable; foreigners often find that they make friends with them quickly. Northerners generally have hearty appetites: the visitor to Lancashire or Yorkshire, for instance, may look forward to receiving generous helpings at meal times.

In accent and character the people of the Midlands represent a gradual change from the southern to the northern type of Englishman.

In Scotland the sound denoted by the letter 'R' is generally a strong sound, and 'R' is often pronounced in words in which it would be silent in southern English. In the Highlands and the Western Isles the ancient Scottish language, Gaelic, is still heard—in 1971 some 88,000 people spoke Gaelic. The Scots are said to be a serious, cautious, thrifty people, rather inventive and somewhat mystical. All the Celtic peoples of Britain (the Welsh, the Irish, the Scots) are frequently described as being more 'fiery' than the English. They are of a race that is quite distinct from the English.

The Welsh have preserved their language to a remarkable extent, as you will see in the article on 'Wales—Land of Song'. The English generally look upon the Welsh as an emotional people who are, however, somewhat reticent and difficult to get to know easily.

Ireland is divided into two parts. The six counties of Northern Ireland are still part of Great Britain, though, in normal circumstances, they have their own Parliament. The majority of people in Northern Ireland are Protestants. The Republic of Ireland,

Top Tossing the caber an unusual Scottish sport.
Bottom Irish dancing

which covers the larger part of the island, is a separate state, not part of Great Britain. The population is predominantly Catholic. Irish, often called Erse, is a form of Gaelic. It was in danger of dying out, but when the territory of the Republic became independent (the Irish 'Free State', 1922), Erse was revived, and is now the official first language of the Republic, English being the second. The Irish are known for their charm and vivacity, as well as for the beauty of the Irish girls.

A   Vocabulary

1   What is the difference between *people* and *a people*?

2   What is the adjective corresponding to *variety*?

3   Explain these expressions.
to be annoyed, predominantly, a region, to revive, apt to, to look upon, thrifty, a helping

4   Complete the following list.

Country	Person	Adjective	The people as a whole
England	an Englishman	English	the English
Wales			
Ireland			
Scotland			
Britain			

5   Is there a difference between *farther* and *further*?

6   Give the different meanings of *speech* in:
   a The Prime Minister made a great speech.
   b Speech distinguishes men from animals.

7   What does *vivacity* mean, and what is the adjective corresponding to it?

8   What is the difference between *charm* and *a charm*?

9   Give the meanings of these expressions.
to look upon, to look down upon

B   Questions on 'The peoples of Britain'

1   Are all people in Britain 'English'?

2   Do all English people speak English of the same type?

3 What sort of English do foreigners generally learn?
4 What qualities are the people of the North of England said to have?
5 Who pronounce 'R' more often, the English or the Scots?
6 Do the Celtic peoples and the English belong to the same race?
7 Mention one feature of the Welsh character.
8 Is the island of Ireland all one state?
9 What is the position of the Irish language (Erse) today?
10 In what part of Ireland are there fewer Catholics than Protestants?

C Grammar

1 In the following sentences insert the verb (given in brackets) in the infinitive (with or without 'to') or the present participle form, as required.

a I hope . . . . (see) you again soon.
b I look forward to . . . . (meet) you again soon.
c He keeps on . . . . (say) the same thing.
d He had difficulty in . . . . (pronounce) the word.
e We enjoyed . . . . (listen) to the Irish pipe-music.
f My friend wanted . . . . (eat) some good Yorkshire roast-beef.
g My Welsh friend used . . . . (sing) 'Land of My Fathers' with much feeling.
h You will soon get used to . . . . (eat) a full English breakfast.
i We are all apt to . . . . (make) spelling mistakes.
j He believes in . . . . (keep) cheerful as much as possible.
k It is not difficult . . . . (learn) a little English.
l . . . . (learn) a foreign language is a useful pastime.
m How careless of you! You have let the canary . . . . (get) out of its cage.
n At the frontier they made us . . . . (show) our passports.
o I should like . . . . (see) that film again.
p They allowed us . . . . (visit) the old castle.
q My friend soon learnt . . . . (speak) English quite well.

    r He was made . . . . (repeat) the word he found difficult . . . .
(say).

    s I am used to . . . . (answer) foreigners' questions.

2 Insert the correct preposition in the following sentences.

    a He referred . . . . the custom . . . . singing 'God Save
the Queen' at the end of a theatrical performance.

    b This is a secret . . . . you and me.

    c The old man spoke . . . . us . . . . Erse.

    d We had a long conversation . . . . them.

    e The old Welshman talked . . . . us . . . . broken English.

    f I enjoyed my talk . . . . the old shepherd.

    g A sudden change . . . . a warm climate to a cold one is
unpleasant.

D Write an essay on the people or peoples of your own
country, trying to bring out their differences.

In the Highlands

The drive from England to Scotland provides the traveller with many pleasant changes of scenery. As it is a fairly long journey, it is good to be able to travel with a friend who can take turns with you at the wheel.

A patriotic Scotsman travelling with an English friend may tell him he is going to see, in the Highlands, the finest scenery in the world. This may sound exaggerated, but on arriving in the Highlands most people readily agree that the scenery is indeed magnificent.

The Highlands are, as the name implies, the hilly or mountainous region of the country; they form the greater part of the western half of Scotland north of Glasgow.

On the first night in Scotland a tourist may choose to put up at a hotel in the little town of Callander, which is known as one of 'the Gateways to the Highlands'. On the following day he can set out to see the various lakes, or rather 'lochs', in the neighbourhood,

Highland cattle – a shaggy breed you may see all over the Highlands of Scotland

and will be delighted with the wild and romantic aspect of the countryside. When he returns to his hotel he will be glad to eat a copious 'high tea'. This is a meal which, in Scotland and many parts of northern England, takes the place of tea and dinner. It consists of one substantial course, such as one would have at dinner, followed by bread-and-butter, with jam or honey, and some kind of cake or cakes; tea is drunk with the meal, which is taken at about six o'clock in the evening. One has a light supper late in the evening.

The next morning many tourists journey on to the west coast, passing on their way Loch Lomond, one of the largest and most famous of the Scottish lakes (these are called 'lochs', with the exception of the Lake of Menteith, not far from Glasgow.) The road twists and turns, dips and climbs, but is not dangerous. The greatest hazard is the black-faced sheep: these animals are as active and impudent as goats, and frequently wander recklessly into the road. The tourist may also see a herd of long-haired Highland cattle, which look savage but are no more so than ordinary cattle. Eventually the road runs parallel with the sea, along a coastline fringed with little islands and made ragged with rocky bays and the deep inlets that are also called 'lochs'.

A   Vocabulary

1   What is meant by *to take turns*?
2   What wheel is meant in the expression *to take turns at the wheel*?
3   What are the names given to the meat of these animals? cows, sheep, pigs, calves, deer
4   What is the opposite of a *reckless* person?
5   What is the difference between a *wild* animal and a *savage* animal?
6   What is the meaning of *eventually*?
7   'Deep water' . . . . what is the opposite of *deep*?
8   On what might one find a *fringe*?
9   'A *herd* of cattle' . . . . and a . . . . of sheep.
10 Make sentences using the following verbal expressions. to put up, to get to, to take turns, to set out, to go on

B   Questions on 'In the Highlands'

1   Does it take long to drive from England to Scotland?
2   What may make a long journey less tiring for a driver?
3   What sort of country are the Highlands?
4   Where might a tourist stay on his first night in Scotland?
5   What is meant by *high tea*?
6   What do Scotsmen often have in place of dinner?
7   What is the road to the west coast like?
8   Why are Highland sheep sometimes dangerous for motorists?
9   What other animals may one see?
10   What is a *loch*?

C   Grammar

1   Give the past tense and the past and present participles of these verbs.
drive, run, imply, see, eat, find, take, dip, tell, hire
2   Give the adverbs corresponding to the following.
appropriate, patriotic, romantic, inevitable, ordinary
3   Complete the following sentences with *one* word only in each case.
    a   This soup tastes ....
    b   That girl looks ....
    c   The traveller seemed ....
    d   The news sounds ....
    e   This fish smells ....
4   Complete the following sentences.
    a   I told him that .... the day before.
    b   I told him what ....
    c   I told him that the next day we ....
    d   My pessimistic friend said that ....
    e   I expected that the sheep ....
    f   The thief took what ....
    g   .... what the weather will be like tomorrow.
    h   .... that it is called the 'gateway to the Highlands'.
    i   .... that the scenery was magnificent.

D   Complete the following sentences. Insert *one* word in each blank space. The word must be an adjective or an adverb, and is to be found in the text of 'In the Highlands'.

1   Some Scotsmen are so . . . . that they claim that England is a peninsula to the south of Scotland.
2   My uncle has left me a . . . . amount of money.
3   It is . . . . to play with fire.
4   . . . . we shall all die.
5   He is a badly brought up, ... boy.
6   You should think before you act, and not do things . . . . .
7   He dug a . . . . hole and buried the treasure in it.
8   I felt very sleepy after my . . . . meal.

E   Write an account of a trip you have made in your own country.

Edinburgh

Edinburgh, the capital of Scotland, is a fine old city built partly in the valley of the River Leith and partly on the rolling hills which surround it. The city is dominated by the castle, an ancient fortress standing on the summit of a massive rock, which has been the scene of many battles and sieges throughout centuries of Scottish history. Today what remains of the original castle is preserved as a museum piece and a home for military relics.

The road from the castle to the royal palace of Holyroodhouse is known as 'The Royal Mile'. It is a very old thoroughfare running through the oldest part of the city where there are many famous historic houses and narrow lanes called 'closes'. The newer part of the city lies north of the famous Princes Street, which is the widest and most impressive of the many wide streets, elegant squares and imposing terraces that are to be found in Edinburgh.

The trains bringing visitors to Edinburgh run right into the heart of the city. Climbing up the steps from Waverley Station, the visitor is greeted by a blaze of colour in Princes Street Gardens and a splendid view down the mile-long length of Princes Street itself.

Edinburgh, with the Castle, the Scott Memorial and Princes Street

The grey stone buildings that line one side of Princes Street have been described as 'a series of palaces'; they are, in fact, department stores and shops. In some shops you can see beautiful displays of Scottish tartans and woollens, and tempting arrangements of shortbread, Edinburgh rock and, of course, Scotch whisky. About half way along Princes Street is the tallest spire in the city—a monumental memorial to Sir Walter Scott—and a little farther on is the Floral Clock. This unique clock, made entirely of growing flowers, is always in full bloom during the Edinburgh Festival.

For three weeks every summer, Edinburgh is alive with exhilarated festival-goers and performers who come from all over the world, and the city is gay with flags and decorations. This international festival of the arts fills every theatre, concert hall, exhibition gallery and assembly room with performances of opera, dancing, music, plays, revues, films, puppet shows and recitals, and specially-mounted exhibitions of painting and sculpture. The festival is not limited to indoor activities: every weekday the noise of the city's traffic is lost in the sound of music as the Scottish pipers march along Princes Street with kilts swinging and drums beating. But the most spectacular event of the festival is undoubtedly the military tattoo. This takes place under searchlights on the Castle esplanade—the scene of many executions in the past—with the floodlit castle in the background. Nowhere could one find a natural setting more impressive and appropriate.

A   Vocabulary

1   What sort of hills are *rolling* hills?
2   Define *massive*.
3   What is a *siege*?
4   What is a *relic*?
5   What is a *thoroughfare*? What does the *fare* part of the word mean?
6   Can you suggest a synonym for *imposing* in the phrase 'imposing terraces'?
7   Give a synonym for *heart* in the phrase 'heart of the city'.
8   What is a *'blaze of colour'*?
9   What buildings normally possess *spires*?

10   How does one feel when one is *exhilarated*?
11   What is a *puppet*?
12   What do you do if you *floodlight* a place?

B   Questions on 'Edinburgh'

1   What is the location of the city of Edinburgh?
2   What building dominates the town? What is it used for?
3   Which part of Edinburgh is known as the 'Royal Mile'?
4   Where does the newer part of the city lie and what does it consist of?
5   What two impressive sights greet the visitor as he leaves Waverley station?
6   What can you see in shops in Princes Street?
7   Where is the tallest spire in Edinburgh to be found?
8   When is the Edinburgh Festival held?
9   What sort of festival is it?
10   Mention three activities which go on during the Edinburgh Festival.
11   Which is the city's most spectacular event and where does it take place?

C   Grammar

1   The adjective from *flower* is *floral*. Make adjectives from the following.
music, accident, bloom, coward, pride, child, trouble, love, anger, friend, faith, fear
2   Insert *some* or *any* or a compound word beginning with *some* or *any* in the following sentences.
    a I have . . . . letters for Mr Brown.
    b Have you . . . . letters for me?
    c Has . . . . called to see me?
    d Has . . . . seen my purse . . . . ?
    e Would you like . . . . more meat?
    f Would you like . . . . of these flowers? Please take . . . . if you would.

D   Complete the following sentences.

1   While I was swimming in the lake . . . .
2   If it rains tomorrow . . . .
3   Every day at nine o'clock . . . .
4   Always take a map when . . . .
5   If the sun is not shining I . . . .
6   I was digging while my friend . . . .
7   For the first ten years of my life . . . .
8   For three weeks now I . . . .

E   Describe any visit you have made to an interesting city.

Wales—'Land of song'

On the western side of Britain lies one of the most beautiful parts of the British Isles: the Principality of Wales. The Welsh mountains have a beauty which is rugged and forbidding, but the slopes are as green and fertile as the valleys and provide rich pasture for sheep and cows.

In central and north Wales, farming is the main occupation, but the valleys of south Wales are very heavily industrialised. Here the wealth of the land lies below the surface in rich coal seams, and the mining villages have grown into busy towns around iron and steel foundries, chemical works and oil refineries.

Wales is very popular for holidays. Every year, thousands of people spend their summer holidays at the seaside resorts on the North Wales coast or, if they prefer it, enjoy undisturbed peace and quiet in isolated villages remote from town life. Those who like to be energetic will probably choose Snowdonia. This part of the country round Snowdon, the highest peak in the Welsh mountains (and the second highest in Britain), is ideal for climbing and walking holidays.

Snowdonia.

Wales has been called 'The Land of Song'. The Welsh people are renowned for their good voices and it is rare to find a village without at least one choir competing in an 'eisteddfod' or arts festival. The biggest festival of all is the International Eisteddfod held every year in Llangollen in Clwyd. Singers, dancers, musicians and poets come from all over the world to compete for the awards, often wearing colourful national costume. The Welsh girls contribute to the festival gaiety with their national dress—a tall black hat, a scarlet skirt and a starched white apron. The streets of this small country town bustle with the comings and goings of visitors speaking many languages. One of the foreign languages heard will be English, for in North Wales many of the local people speak Welsh as their native tongue. Today, only about a quarter of the Welsh population speak this ancient language as their first language, although many more who use English can understand Welsh as well, and encourage their children to learn it at school. The Welsh people are proud of being Celtic, different from the Anglo-Saxon English, with an ancient language and a heritage of their own.

An old photograph of the Llanderfel Village Choir who sang to Queen Victoria in 1889

A   Vocabulary

1   What type of countryside would the word *rugged* be applied to?
2   Can you explain the difference between the verb *to forbid*
and the adjective *forbidding*?
3   What is a *seam* of coal?
4   What takes place in an iron *foundry*?
5   What does *remote* mean?
6   What is a mountain *peak*?
7   What is the opposite of *rare*?
8   What is a *choir*?
9   Can you find another word for *bustle*?
10   What is one's *native* tongue?
11   Explain the term *heritage*.

B   Questions on 'Wales—"Land of song"'

1   In what way does south Wales differ from central and north
Wales?
2   What is the basis of the wealth of south Wales?
3   For what reason do many people go to Wales?
4   State two very different types of holiday one could spend
in Wales.
5   What is the name of the highest mountain in Wales?
6   Why is Wales often called the 'land of song'?
7   What is an eisteddfod?
8   What is the location of the International Eisteddfod? Is it in
Wales?
9   Describe the national costume of Welsh women.
10   What percentage of the population of Wales speaks Welsh?

C   Grammar

1   Use the simple past or the present perfect (simple) in the
following sentences.
   a It was many years ago that I . . . . (meet) him for the
   first time.

  b I . . . . (just, discover) my mistake.
  c Tell me what you . . . . (do) during the holidays.
  d I . . . . (just, finish), dressing and am now ready to go.
  e He . . . . (be) fast asleep for three hours now.
  f He . . . . (be) fast asleep when we arrived.
 2 Fill in the omitted prepositions in the following sentences.
  a I don't like my present job; it's getting me . . . .
  b Life is cheaper in the country than in the town, we can live . . . . practically nothing.
  c I see my friend frequently as he lives quite close . . . . me.
  d One should never laugh . . . . the misfortunes of others.
  e He read the order . . . . the men . . . . the piece of paper in his hand.
  f He jumped . . . . joy when he heard the good news.
  g When the bandit pointed the gun . . . . me I shook . . . . fright.
  h I passed . . . . your house yesterday as I was going . . . . school.

D Replace the words in italics in the following sentences with an expression containing the word *set*.

 1 A statue was *erected* in the market place.
 2 The runner *established* a world record.
 3 He *went into* business as a greengrocer.
 4 *Write* your impressions at once.
 5 At what time shall we *leave*?

E Write an essay on a famous event that takes place in your native country.

Do-it-yourself

Some people would say that the Englishman's home is no longer his castle; that it has become his workshop. This is partly because the average Englishman is keen on working with his hands and partly because he feels, for one reason or another, that he must do for himself many household jobs for which, some years ago, he would have hired professional help. The main reason for this is a financial one: the high cost of labour has meant that builders' and decorators' costs have reached a level which makes them prohibitive for house-proud Englishpeople of modest means. So, if they wish to keep their houses looking bright and smart, they have to tackle some of the repairs and decorating themselves. As a result, there has grown up in the post-war years what is sometimes referred to as the 'Do-It-Yourself Movement'.

The 'Do-It-Yourself Movement' began with home decorating but has since spread into a much wider field. Nowadays there seem to be very few things that cannot be made by the 'do-it-yourself' method. A number of magazines and handbooks exist to show hopeful handymen of all ages just how easy it is to build anything from a coffee table to a fifteen foot (4.5 metres) sailing dinghy. All you need, it seems, is a hammer and a few nails. You follow the simple instructions step-by-step and, before you know where you are, the finished article stands before you, complete in every detail.

Unfortunately, alas, it is not always quite as simple as it sounds! Many a budding 'do-it-yourselfer' has found to his cost that one cannot learn a skilled craftsman's job overnight. How quickly one realises, when doing it oneself, that a job which takes the skilled man an hour or so to complete takes the amateur handyman five or six at least. And then there is the question of tools. The first thing the amateur learns is that he must have the right tools for

An advertisement from a Do-it-yourself magazine

the job. But tools cost money. There is also the wear and tear on the nerves. It is not surprising then that many people have come to the conclusion that the expense of paying professionals to do the work is, in the long run, more economical than 'doing it oneself'.

A Vocabulary

1   Explain the colloquial expression *to be keen on*.
2   What is the difference between a *builder* and a *decorator*?
3   Find one or more synonyms for *smart*.
4   Explain the meaning of *prohibitive* cost.
5   What are *modest* means? To what is the term *modest* normally applied?
6   Find an alternative for the verb *to tackle*.
7   Can you distinguish between a *magazine* and a *handbook*?
8   What is a *handyman*?
9   What does *budding* mean as used in the passage? To what would the term *budding* normally apply?
10   Find an alternative expression for *in the long run*.

B Questions on 'Do-it-yourself'

1   Why would some people say that the Englishman's home has become his workshop?
2   Give one important reason why many Englishmen now 'do it themselves'.
3   When did the 'do-it-yourself' movement grow up?
4   In what field did it begin?
5   What have many do-it-yourself enthusiasts learned about the time it takes to do it yourself?
6   What is the first thing the amateur learns?
7   What conclusion do many 'do-it-yourselfers' come to in the long run?

C Grammar

1 Put the following sentences into the passive.
   a The officer led his men to victory.
   b The centre-forward scored the winning goal of the match.
   c He gave me a glass of his best wine.
   d You ought to clean your teeth every morning.
   e He papered three walls before he discovered that the
   wallpaper was upside down.
   f Decorators always clean surfaces before painting.
   g The workmen put the building up in three weeks.
2 Complete the expressions in which *run* is used in the
following sentences.
   a The pedestrian was run . . . . by a car.
   b The author of this book ran . . . . from home at an early
   age.
   c I ran . . . . an old friend of mine yesterday.
   d I have been overworking lately and I feel very run . . . .
   as a result.
   e Run . . . . your lives!
   f As the car slowly stopped I realised that I had run . . . .
   of petrol.

D Put each of the following expressions into a sentence to
show that you know its meaning.

1 to look up
2 to look for
3 to look at
4 to look up to
5 to look down on
6 to look out
7 to look sharp

E Describe in detail how you would furnish and decorate
any room in the house.

Public libraries

Britain is very fortunate in its system of public lending-libraries. In this respect we can do no better than quote from 'Britain: An Official Handbook' (published by Her Majesty's Stationery Office; a very valuable reference book):

'Britain is served by a complete network of public libraries, administered by local public library authorities. These libraries have a total stock of some 115 million books (not including the libraries in publicly maintained schools).

Qualified and specialist staff are available for consultation in all but the smallest service points. About one-third of the total population are members of public libraries.' This lending and reference library service is, with some limitations, free.

Public libraries not only lend books, music scores and records, but also provide special libraries for, among others, children, patients in hospitals and prisoners, and they engage in many kinds of extension activities, such as play readings, lectures, film shows, music circles and co-operation in adult education.

The growth of public libraries in Britain goes back to 1850, when the Public Libraries Act (largely due to the work of the Scottish M.P., William Ewart) authorised municipalities to levy a small rate for the financing of libraries. Today, the local library usually provides a reading room (with newspapers and magazines), a reference library and a lending library. For the use of these facilities no charge is made. Through regional co-operation and that of the National Central Library it is possible to borrow books that may not be available at the local library.

Schools, universities, technical institutes, professional associations and similar organizations also maintain libraries of books for reference or for borrowing. There are, too, various private lending libraries.

The greatest and most famous library in Britain is that of the British Museum (now part of the British Library created in 1973), which possesses over six million books. A copy of every book, magazine, newspaper, etc., published in Great Britain must be sent to the British Museum. The Reading Room of the Museum is famous for the number of scholars and notabilities who have studied in it. The British Museum Library is not, by the way, a lending library!

The second best-known library in Britain is the Bodleian Library

The Reading Room of the British Museum has its own unique atmosphere.

at Oxford (over two million volumes). The National Library of Scotland (about two million volumes), Cambridge University Library (over two million volumes), the National Library of Wales (more than one and a quarter million volumes) are also famous, and may claim a copy of every new work published in Britain. There is also a National Library for the Blind, with over three hundred thousand volumes in a specially embossed type.

A Vocabulary

1 Give an antonym for *private* (adjective).
2 Explain the meaning of the following.
to quote, to finance, a reference library, available,
a notability, to claim, a municipality, stationery, a lecture

3 Explain the meaning of *score* in these sentences.
   a The violinist had a music score in front of him.
   b He bought a score of eggs.
   c The score was three goals to nil.
   d There were scores of people there.
4 Explain the meaning of *rate* in these sentences.
   a The rates in this part of London are high.
   b What is the rate of pay for the job?
5 Insert the verb *lend* or *borrow* as needed in these sentences.
   a I will . . . . you the book, if you promise to take care of it.
   b I was penniless, so I had to . . . . fifty pence.
   c The abbreviation 'R.S.V.P.' (meaning 'Please reply') is . . . .
   from French.
   d Don't . . . . that fellow a penny!
   What does Mark Antony (in Shakespeare's 'Julius Cæsar')
   mean when he says: 'Friends, Romans, countrymen, *lend
   me your ears*'? Would you use this expression?
6 State what is meant by *scholar* in these sentences.
The scholars at Greylands College wear a dark grey uniform.
He is an excellent teacher but no great scholar.
7 Explain the meaning of *scholarship* in these sentences.
Professor Jowett was a man of great scholarship.
Jack is a bright boy and will certainly gain a scholarship.

B   Questions on 'Public Libraries'

1 Are British public lending libraries well-organized?
2 Are there many public library authorities in Britain?
3 Do people in Britain borrow many books?
4 Do people have to pay to borrow books from a library?
5 Name some things that public libraries provide, apart from
books.
6 How are public libraries paid for?
7 What three facilities does one usually find in a public
library?
8 What institutions, besides public libraries, have books for
reference?
9 Why is the British Museum Reading Room famous?

C Grammar

1 Make two sentences with each of the following words; in one sentence use the word as an adjective and in the other sentence as a noun.

savage, private, public, native, cold

2 Insert *among, with, of, up, in, into, without, for, out* as needed in the following sentences.

   a Jack wants to be a sailor when he grows . . . .
   b I hope you will grow . . . . that bad habit.
   c The various libraries co-operate . . . . one another.
   d . . . . his books he has several valuable volumes.
   e The house is provided . . . . all modern facilities.
   f He works hard as he has to provide . . . . a large family.
   g The museum is famous . . . . its Greek statues.
   h The little lamb grew . . . . a fine ram.
   i This library is . . . . doubt world-famous.
   j Professor Richards is engaged . . . . research.

3 Give the nouns corresponding to the following.

curious, to grow, to refer, to organise, possible, to publish, famous, to claim, to quote, to extend

D Write an essay on 'The sort of books that I like', or 'Some books that I like' (Explaining why you like these books).

The daily newspapers

The British are the most voracious newspaper readers in the world. They read newspapers at breakfast; they walk to the bus reading a newspaper; they read a newspaper on the bus, as they go to work; and on the way back home, after work, they are engrossed in an evening newspaper.

There are many 'morning papers', both national and provincial. The most famous is *The Times*. Contrary to what many foreigners believe, this is not a government newspaper. The various newspapers usually have their own views on politics, but they are not organs of the political parties, with the exception of the Communist *Morning Star*. The Labour Party and the Trades Union Congress no longer have a daily newspaper to represent them.

A newspaper seller outside a London tube station

Bold headlines and a variety of photographs are features of the British press. Some newspapers, such as the sober *Daily Telegraph* and *The Times* (which belong to the 'quality press') use photographs sparingly. The more 'popular' newspapers, using the small or 'tabloid' format, such as the *Daily Express,* the *Daily Mail,* the *Daily Mirror* and the *Sun,* use pictures extensively and also run strip-cartoons and humorous drawings, some of which present striking pictorial comment on politics.

Besides offering features common to newspapers all over the world, British newspapers specialize in pages devoted to criticism of the arts and. a woman's page. One feature found in many foreign newspapers is missing in British papers: the serial.

Nearly all papers pay special attention to the reporting of sport and athletics. The evening newspapers (the first editions of which appear in the morning!) are often bought because the purchaser wants to know the winner of a race, or to get a good tip for a race that is still to be run.

There is no censorship of the press in Britain (except in war-time), though of course all newspapers—like private persons—are responsible for what they publish, and can be sued for libel for publishing articles that go beyond the bounds of decency, or for 'contempt of court' (e.g. calling a man a murderer while he is still being tried). Such lawsuits are infrequent.

A   Vocabulary

1   Give a word or phrase similar in meaning to the words
in italic in the following sentences.
  a The shark is a *voracious* fish.
  b We *rarely* see foreigners here.
  c Such headlines are a *feature* of our newspapers.
  d Mr Wilson *runs* a large hotel.
  e I don't think that remark was very *humorous*.
  f This is a *common* prejudice, at least among ignorant
  people.
  g Don't use such *common* language.
  h He *bought* a new car.
  i He is very *popular* with his colleagues.
  j The photographs are *distributed* throughout these pages.
2   What is meant by a *national* newspaper?
3   Explain what is meant by the following.
  a The Trades Union Congress (T.U.C.)
  b The Labour Party
  c Format
  d A strip-cartoon
  e A serial (What is the meaning of the homophone
  a *cereal*?)
  f A *tip* for a race (In what other sense may a *tip* be used?)
  g Censorship
  h A murderer
  i Libel (What is the word used for a similar offence that is
  committed by *speaking*?)
4   Give the meaning of the following frequent abbreviations.
e.g. i.e. a.m. p.m. A.D. B.C. c/o viz. do. M.P.
5   What do *the former* and *the latter* mean? Write a sentence
containing both words.
6   What are the nouns corresponding to the following
adjectives?
provincial, voracious, famous, various, sober, popular, humorous,
special, private, decent
7   What is the meaning of *striking* in the phrase 'striking
pictorial comment'?

B   Questions on 'The daily newspapers'

1   Do the British read newspapers very much?
2   Is *The Times* a government newspaper?
3   Name two characteristic features of British newspapers.
4   To what category of newspapers do *The Times* and the *Daily Telegraph* belong?
5   How do newspapers sometimes offer criticism of politics?
6   What feature of many foreign newspapers is lacking in British newspapers?
7   When do the evening papers first appear?
8   When is the press censored in Britain?
9   What should a newspaper not publish, if it does not wish to be sued?

C   Grammar

1   Insert the correct preposition in the following sentences.
    a My friend was engrossed . . . . a novel.
    b This is contrary . . . . the law.
    c It is connected . . . . the T.U.C.
    d I made no comment . . . . the situation.
    e This feature is common . . . . most newspapers.
    f The contrary . . . . black is white.
    g That is the opposite . . . . the truth.
    h His views . . . . religion are sound.
    i From there we shall have a lovely view . . . . the river.
    j He specializes . . . . South American stamps.
2   Give the past tense and the past and present participles of these verbs.
believe, prefer, deal, bring, strike

D   Write an essay on newspapers in your country or on the influence of the press.

More about the Press

Besides the daily newspapers, there are a number of Sunday newspapers, many of which are connected with the 'dailies', though not run by the same editor and staff. The Sunday papers are larger than the daily papers and usually contain a greater proportion of articles concerned with comment and general information rather than news. The national daily and Sunday papers have enormous circulations (the largest in the world) running into several millions of readers in certain cases. The economics of newspaper publishing in Britain and in particular their reliance on advertising revenue have, in recent years, led to the closing-down of several newspapers; their circulations would have been considered large in many other countries, but they were insufficient to ensure the life of a national newspaper in Britain. Of the Sunday papers, the *Observer* and the *Sunday Times* are the best known; their literary and artistic reviews are particularly prized, especially among the more highbrow members of the community. Several Sunday newspapers now publish a magazine supplement in colour.

Some of the daily and the Sunday newspapers are at times criticised for being too sensational and devoting too much space to reporting murders and other crimes.

It is a regrettable fact that the number of magazines of a literary or political nature has declined since the war. This has probably been caused by the ever-wider use of radio and television. The most flourishing magazines are those published for women. Their covers are designed to catch the eye, and they certainly succeed in doing so! They offer their readers articles on cookery, fashion, needlework, knitting and many other matters of feminine interest. They also provide advice to those in love, 'your fate foretold by the stars', and stories of romance with handsome heroes. Some women's magazines also include serious articles of more general interest.

The visitor who looks at the magazines displayed in a large bookstall such as one may find in an important railway station will notice that there is a wide variety of technical or semi-technical publications. There are magazines for the motorist, the farmer, the gardener, the nurse, the wireless enthusiast, and many others.

There are many local and regional newspapers. It is customary in Britain for a newsagent to deliver the morning papers to his

The morning newspaper round

customers for a small extra payment; this service is usually performed by boys and girls who want to earn some pocket-money.

A Vocabulary

1 What is the difference between an *editor* and a *publisher*?
2 What is meant by the *circulation* of a newspaper?
3 What is meant by 'the *economics* of newspaper publishing'? Explain the difference between *economic* and *economical*.
4 By means of a synonym or a phrase, explain what is meant by the following.
a review, to prize, to decline, to flourish, to catch the eye, highbrow, to foretell
5 Give the meanings of these phrases.
a romance, a novel, a short story, an autobiography, a biography

6   What is the adjective meaning 'concerned with cookery'?

7   *Murder* is a crime. Give the names of the following illegal activities.

    a Illegally burning down a house

    b Breaking into a house to steal

    c Telling lies when one has sworn to tell the truth

    d Stealing a person, with a view to getting money for setting the person free again

    e Killing oneself

8   What is the verb meaning *to make a criticism*? What is the name used for a person who does so?

9   Explain the difference between a *magazine* and a *newspaper*.

B   Questions on 'More about the Press'

1   Are the Sunday papers the same as the daily papers?

2   What is special about the content of Sunday papers?

3   Why have several newspapers had to close down in recent years?

4   For what is the *Observer* well known?

5   What is the press sometimes blamed for?

6   What has caused a decline in the number of literary and political magazines?

7   What magazines are selling best?

8   Name some features of these best-selling magazines.

9   Where may one find a good selection of magazines?

10   Why do many boys and girls deliver morning newspapers?

C   Grammar

1   The word *information* has no plural. Find other words that have no plural, e.g. the words for the following.

    a Chairs, tables, beds, etc.

    b Valises, trunks, etc.

    c Counsel, opinion

    d The latest information

    e Amusement (a word of three letters.)

2 Write the following in full.

135,   200,000,   4,625,823,   1,600, $\frac{1}{100}$.

3 Write a sentence with each of the following words correctly used in its plural form.

dozen, score (i.e. 20), hundred, thousand, million

4 Write a sentence containing *its* and another with *it's*.

5 *Daily, hourly, weekly, monthly, yearly,* are used as adjectives or as adverbs (e.g. A daily paper is published daily). Find words of similar grammatical behaviour for the following.

the opposite of slow, the opposite of soft, sufficient or sufficiently

6 Insert *probably* or *likely* correctly in the following sentences.

   a It isn't . . . . that it will rain today.

   b I shall . . . . see him tomorrow.

7 Complete the following sentences.

   a It is a pity that . . . .

   b It is fortunate that . . . .

   c It was nice of you to . . . .

   d It is a shame that . . . .

   e It is amazing how . . . .

8 Re-write the following sentences in the passive voice.

   a A clever man edits that newspaper.

   b Highbrows do not read this comic magazine.

   c Our foreign correspondent has reported an improvement in the situation.

   d One of our reporters will interview the actor at the airport.

   e The 'Daily Messenger' reported the facts accurately.

D Write an account of a burglary that you imagine has occurred at your chemist's, jeweller's or butcher's.

London's parks

One thing about London which every visitor from abroad admires is the large number of parks. These 'lungs' of London, as they have been called, are like green islands of peace and quiet in the middle of a noisy sea. They play an important part in helping to form the city's character.

The best-known parks are, of course, the central ones: St James's Park, Hyde Park, Regent's Park, and Kensington Gardens. They have many attractions. Hyde Park has the Serpentine, a little lake, where, if one feels inclined, one may take a swim or go for a row, and Speakers' Corner where one may get up and say anything (or almost anything!) one pleases. In Regent's Park there are the Zoo and the Open-Air Theatre. Kensington Gardens has the Round Pond where 'dry land sailors' of all ages sail every kind of model

Children love to feed the ducks on the Serpentine.

yacht. St James's Park boasts a truly elegant lake on which lives a great variety of wild duck. And, apart from these individual attractions, each park has a greater or lesser expanse of well-kept grass. Here, in fine weather, can be seen hundreds of lucky people who have escaped for a while from the noise and bustle of the town; some sitting on chairs, some lying full length on the ground, some strolling aimlessly around.

But the central parks of London are not necessarily the most popular. Every district of London has its parks, great or small. In the north there is Hampstead Heath, famous for its summer and winter fairs. In the south there is Richmond Park, where deer and sheep still roam and where one can get the impression of being deep in the country. In the south, too, are the Botanical Gardens at Kew, where almost every kind of tree and plant is carefully tended, in large greenhouses or in the open air. Just over Chelsea Bridge, along the south bank of the Thames, is Battersea Park, one of London's largest, complete with its Pleasure Gardens and Fun-Fair. In the east, there is the large Victoria Park and a host of smaller ones.

And so one could go on. Even for a Londoner it is difficult to know and enjoy them all. The visitor to the city may be confident that wherever he is, he is not far away from a park of some description which waits to offer him the same pleasures and relaxations that it does to the Londoner.

A Vocabulary

1 What is a *lung*?
2 The men who look after the parks are called *park-keepers*. How many other words can you think of which are formed with the suffix 'keeper'?
3 What is the opposite of *best-known* in the phrase 'the best-known parks'?
4 Find a phrase or word meaning the same as *elegant* and *expanse* (used in paragraph two of the passage).
5 'Bustle' is a word whose sound suggests its meaning. (Such a word is called *onomatopoeic*.) Can you think of half-a-dozen other common onomatopoeic words?

6   What is the opposite of the following?
well-kept, carefully, difficult, far, pleasure, confident, lucky, forwards
7   What does *aimless* mean?

B   Questions on 'London's parks'

1   Which aspect of London do visitors admire?
2   Why, do you think, are the parks called London's *lungs*?
3   What exercise would you find people taking in Hyde Park in the summer?
4   What is Speakers' Corner?
5   What do people use the Round Pond in Kensington Gardens for?
6   What have the people in the parks managed to escape from?
7   What, in Richmond Park, gives one the impression of being in the country?
8   Where is Battersea Park?
9   What is Hampstead Heath noted for?
10 Where are London's best-known parks situated?

C   Grammar

1   Give the adjectives formed from the following nouns.
peace, quiet, theatre, flower, sheep, pleasure, knowledge, beauty, calm
2   Insert *since* or *for* in the following sentences.
   a I had been rowing on the lake .... two o'clock.
   b I had not been swimming .... two years.
   c I haven't been in the park .... I saw you last.
   d We were waiting by the Round Pond .... two hours.
   e The flowers in the park had bloomed .... I was there last.
   f It is a long time .... I saw a performance at the Open-Air Theatre.
   g .... a long time we waited to get into the Fun-Fair.
   h I have been walking round the gardens .... twenty minutes.

3 Put the adverbs or adverbial phrases in brackets in their
proper place in the following sentences.
  a We go for a walk in the park. (frequently)
  b The flowers blossomed. (beautifully; in the spring)
  c We meet on the way to work. (often; early in the
  morning)
  d I do not swim. (often; nowadays)
  e I like to sit in the park. (all day; quietly)
  f He prefers swimming to working. (naturally)
  g I have to spend most of my time working. (unfortunately)
  h They like to row round the lake. (slowly; at sunset)

D   Answer the following questions *with a complete sentence.*

  a Do you like to walk in the park?
  b Have you ever rowed on a lake?
  c Are there any parks in your home town?
  d Is one allowed to walk on the grass?
  e How often do you go to the park?
  f Would you like to visit an open-air theatre?
  g Do you think you could teach someone to swim?
  h Where do you go to find peace and quiet?
  i Has sailing model boats ever been a pastime of yours?
  j Which do you prefer, the town or the country?

E   Write a description of a walk round your favourite park or
open space.

Wild life in Britain

There are no longer any really dangerous wild mammals in Britain, except the wild cat, occasionally found in the depths of Scottish forests. The wolf died out several centuries ago and there are no bears or wild boars, as in some parts of continental Europe. Our largest wild animal is the stag, for wild deer are found in Scotland and in south-west England. More or less tame deer are kept on many big estates and in big parks, such as Richmond Park near London. Deer are shy beasts but, like almost any wild animal, will attack a man in defence of their young, and an angry stag is a dangerous creature, especially if he has his full antlers.

Foxes are found all over Britain, though chiefly in England. They are still hunted with hounds, and deer are also hunted, but many people are against blood-sports, which will perhaps be forbidden one day. The rabbit, a natural prey of the fox, used to infest the countryside literally in millions. However, an epidemic of a terrible disease (myxomatosis) wiped out vast numbers of rabbits although rabbits are becoming more numerous again now. As a consequence, foxes take an even greater interest in domestic poultry, and are of course much disliked by farmers. The hare, the rabbit's 'cousin', is still fairly frequent. Two small bloodthirsty animals, the stoat and the weasel (found more or less all over Britain), also prey on rabbits as well as on other small animals.

The badger, whose hairs provide, it is said, the best shaving-brushes, comes out at night and is useful because he eats slugs, snails, and other garden pests. So also does the hedgehog, which is common in the countryside and in gardens all over the country, and unfortunately is often run over when crossing a road.

A badger coming out of its 'sett' (burrow) at night

Top A fox at night
Bottom Some people put out a saucer of milk for hedgehogs.

A blue-tit feeding on nuts

Only two snakes are found in Britain; both are small. The grass-snake is harmless but the adder is poisonous, though its bite is rarely fatal. There are no adders in Ireland.

As regards fishes, there are various species of fresh-water fishes and angling is a nationwide pastime, whether in lakes and rivers or in the sea, where there are also many kinds of fishes. Pollution of both inland waters and the sea is being slowly (perhaps too slowly) brought under control. Trout and salmon are present in many rivers, particularly in Scotland. Fishermen grumble about the quantities of fish eaten by seals and otters, and concern has been expressed about the possible extermination of these animals.

Birds are numerous and the Royal Society for the Protection of Birds does much for their preservation. It manages a large number of nature reserves, amongst other activities. Many birds are protected by law, especially the rarer species, such as the eagle and the osprey. Our chief song-birds are the nightingale and the blackbird. Owls help to keep down the mouse population. There are more kinds of birds in Britain than can be enumerated here but let us mention the pretty robin redbreast, a frequent character on Christmas cards. Of sea-birds the most common are the various kinds of gulls.

A   Vocabulary

1   Give the adjective and the verb corresponding to the noun *depth*.

2   Which is longer, *several centuries* or *many centuries*?

3   Give a synonym and an opposite for *shy*.

4   Stags have *antlers* on their heads. What do cows and goats have?

5   Give an opposite for *to forbid*.

6   What is an *epidemic*? Can you name an illness that may be an epidemic for human beings?

7   What is the meaning of *to run over* (as in 'run over when crossing a road')?

8   If a bite is *fatal,* what happens to the person bitten?

9   What does an *angler* hope to do?

10   Give a synonym for *to grumble.*

B   Questions on 'Wild life in Britain'

1   If you wanted to see a wild cat in Britain today, where would you go?

2   What may make a stag attack a man?

3   Do all British people approve of hunting stags and foxes?

4   Why are there now relatively few rabbits in Britain?

5   Why do farmers dislike foxes?

6   In what ways is the badger useful to man?

7   Who probably kill seals and otters, and why?

8   What steps are taken in Britain to prevent the extermination of birds?

9   Why is the robin called 'redbreast'?

10   Where would you expect to see gulls?

C   Grammar

1   Supply the missing prepositions.
   a There are no wild bears . . . . Britain.
   b All . . . . Britain one can find many kinds of birds.

c The man was so tired that he slept all . . . . the night.
d The fox preys . . . . rabbits and other small animals.
e More steps must be taken . . . . pollution.
f My friend often goes fishing . . . . trout.
g Deer live mainly . . . . grass.
h There is a society that takes care . . . . wild birds.
i Badgers are active . . . . night.
j We have mentioned only a few . . . . the wild animals of Britain.

2 Insert the verbs, given in brackets, in the past simple tense.
a My friend . . . . a tame otter in his garden. (keep)
b We . . . . a dead hedgehog on the road. (find)
c The stag . . . . the foolish tourist. (attack)
d Parliament . . . . cruel sports. (forbid)
e The fox . . . . several of the farmer's chickens. (take)
f The adder . . . . the boy in the leg. (bite)
g The farmer . . . . a pheasant. (shoot)
h The old owl . . . . several mice. (catch)
i He . . . . home a sparrow with a broken wing. (bring)
j The blackbird . . . . back to its nest. (fly)

D Write a short essay on one of the following subjects.
1 The preservation of wild life
2 Wild life in your own country
3 Wild birds and beasts in towns

London art galleries

On the north side of Trafalgar Square, famous for its monument to Admiral Nelson ('Nelson's Column'), its fountains and its hordes of pigeons, there stands a long, low building in classic style. This is the National Gallery, which contains Britain's best-known collection of pictures. The collection was begun in 1824, with the purchase of thirty-eight pictures that included Hogarth's satirical 'Marriage à la Mode' series, and Titian's 'Venus and Adonis'.

The National Gallery is rich in paintings by Italian masters such as Raphael, Correggio, and Veronese, and it contains pictures representative of all European schools of art such as works by Rembrandt, Rubens, Van Dyck, Murillo, El Greco, and nineteenth century French masters. Many visitors are especially attracted to Velasquez' 'Rokeby Venus' and Leonardo da Vinci's 'Virgin of the Rocks'.

On sunny days, students and other young people are often to be seen having a sandwich lunch on the portico of the Gallery, overlooking Trafalgar Square. Admission to the Gallery is free, as is the case with other British national galleries and museums, which are maintained by money voted by Parliament. Bequests of pictures have been made to the galleries, at times on a generous scale, by private individuals.

Just behind the National Gallery stands the National Portrait Gallery, in which the visitor can see portraits of British monarchs since the reign of Richard II (1377-1399), and of historical celebrities such as Chaucer, Shakespeare, and Cromwell. Many of the pictures are by well-known artists.

The National Gallery of British Art, better known as the Tate Gallery, was given to the nation by a rich sugar merchant, Sir Henry Tate, who had a taste for the fine arts. It overlooks the Thames, not far from the Houses of Parliament. English artists are naturally well represented here, and the Tate also has a range of modern works, including some sculptures, by foreign artists. This, of all the London galleries, is the young people's gallery. It has been stated that three-quarters of its visitors are under twenty-five.

The Wallace Collection at Hertford House was formed by Lord Hertford and his half-brother, Sir Richard Wallace, who inherited the collection, which was given to the nation in 1897 by Sir Richard's widow. There is here a very fine display of weapons and armour,

Top The Hay-Wain by John Constable (1776-1837)
Bottom Edith Sitwell by Wyndham Lewis (1882-1957)

Sculptures in the Tate Gallery.

of pottery, miniatures and sculpture. The first floor of the building contains an admirable assortment of Boucher's pictures, besides excellent examples of the work of Fragonard, to mention only two artists.

On a summer day, a visit to Kenwood House in Kenwood, on the northern side of Hampstead Heath, is well worth while, for here is a small collection of paintings, some by famous painters, that can be viewed in a relatively short time. Afterwards, one can go out into the charming grounds. One may sun oneself on the turf of the spacious lawns, or stroll by the lily-pond and then enter the little wood that half surrounds it. Kenwood House is maintained not by the government but by the Greater London Council.

A Vocabulary

1 Give synonyms for the following.
famous, to purchase, satirical, spacious
2 Explain the meaning of the following.
hordes of pigeons, Italian *masters*, a bequest, to *overlook* the Thames, weapons, armour, a lily-pond, the fine arts
3 What is the difference between a *picture* and a *portrait* and between a *museum* and an *art gallery*?

4　Use the same word, with two different meanings, to complete the following sentences.

    a The Andes are a . . . . of high mountains.
    b The library has a good . . . . of modern novels.

B　Make nine sentences with questions about 'London art galleries'. Here are the answers.

1　On the north side of Trafalgar Square.
2　It began with the buying of thirty-eight pictures.
3　They have a sandwich lunch at the entrance to the National Gallery.
4　You do not have to pay to go in.
5　Private individuals have often left paintings to them.
6　He was rich and he liked the fine arts.
7　It is particularly young people who go there.
8　No, it was made by private persons, Lord Hertford and Sir Richard Wallace.

C　Grammar

1　Insert the verb given in brackets in the correct tense of the passive voice.

    a Many famous pictures . . . . (leave) to our galleries at various times.
    b The National Gallery . . . . (erect) between 1832 and 1838.
    c The national museums . . . . (maintain) out of public funds.
    d The National Portrait Gallery . . . . (situate) just behind the National Gallery.
    e The Wallace Collection . . . . (give) to the nation in 1897.
    f The size of the collection . . . . (increase) recently by generous gifts.
    g The trustees of the gallery hope that more pictures . . . . (give) to it in future.

2　Make sentences containing the following words, used as different parts of speech, as indicated.
purchase (Noun/Verb), representative (Adjective/Noun), vote (Noun/Verb), charm (Noun/Verb), stroll (Noun/Verb)

D　Write an essay on 'My favourite artist and his pictures'.

Spring flowers by Coniston Water in the Lake District.

A typical village street at Lavenham in Suffolk.

Winchester Cathedral at Christmas-time.

The Life Guards riding through Hyde Park, London.

The Queen inspecting the Guardsmen at the annual ceremony of 'Trooping the Colour'.

The Prince and Princess of Wales on the steps of St Paul's Cathedral after their wedding.

The famous London department
store, Harrods, at night.

An old Victorian pub in
the centre of London.

The Dickens Inn, St. Katherine's Dock, London with Tower Bridge in the background.

A country pub in Suffolk.

Traditional Welsh costume at the International Eisteddfod, Llangollen, Wales.

A performance of Shakespeare's play *Much Ado About Nothing* at the Regent's Park Open Air Theatre, London.

Mini-Metro cars on the production line at a British Leyland factory.

The first cast-iron bridge in the world, built in 1777. Ironbridge, Shropshire.

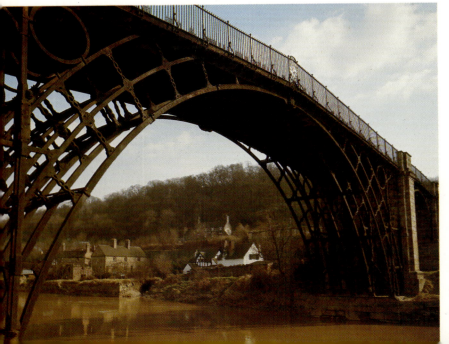

The Houses of Parliament

Close by Westminster Abbey on the riverside stands the Palace of Westminster, generally known as the Houses of Parliament. Although these buildings are in Gothic style, they are not truly historic, for they were built in 1840 on the site of the old Palace which was destroyed by fire in 1834. Parliament consists of two separate chambers whose membership and duties have evolved slowly over centuries: the House of Lords (or Upper House), whose members sit there by hereditary right or conferred privilege (there is an increasing number of life peers, whose titles cease when they die), and the House of Commons, where the elected Members of Parliament sit. Although the Upper House is the larger in membership—more than one thousand peers have the right to attend the sittings—nearly all the legislation is initiated in the House of Commons and presented to the Lords for approval. This is, however, little more than a formality, for the powers of the House of Lords are strictly limited.

The six hundred and fifty elected members of the House of Commons meet in a Chamber which is still sometimes called St Stephen's Chapel. The original chapel where the first parliaments assembled centuries ago was lost in 1834, and the present Chamber is a replica of the one built in 1840 but destroyed during World War II. The members sit on two sides of the Chamber, one side for the Government and the other for the Opposition. Between them sits 'Mr Speaker', who acts as chairman in the debates.

The flag shows that the House is sitting.

The Queen opens Parliament in the House of Lords.

Traditionally, his role was to inform the House of Lords and the monarch of decisions taken by the elected parliament, and as there have been periods in British history when such a duty could be dangerous, the member chosen to be Mr Speaker always accepts the position with the pretence of great reluctance and fear!

It is a privilege of democratic government that anyone may visit the Houses of Parliament and may sit in the Strangers' Gallery, looking down into the House of Commons, to listen to a debate. The Central Lobby entrance hall is usually busy with people coming and going, some just curious to see the inside of the buildings, others wanting to see their own elected M.P. On fine days, the terrace overlooking the river is crowded with small tables where Members can entertain their guests to tea.

The Parliamentary session begins in November and, with recessions at holiday periods (Christmas, Easter and in summer), lasts for about one hundred and sixty days. The sittings begin at 2.30 p.m. from Monday to Thursday and at 11 a.m. on Friday. There is no set finishing time for sittings and if there is urgent business to discuss the sittings may go on until late at night or, indeed, all through the night. All the time Parliament is in session, a flag flies at the top of the Victoria tower, and when the House is still sitting after dark, a light burns over the clock face of Big Ben.

A   Vocabulary

1   Explain the meaning of the following words.
privilege, conferred, initiated, replica, curious, urgent
2   Give the opposite of the following verbs.
destroy, lose, initiate, accept
3   What does 'hereditary right' mean?
4   The House of Lords is called the Upper House. What do you think the House of Commons is called?
5   Give a synonym for the word *rôle*.
6   Distinguish between *reluctance* and *fear*.
7   Find an alternative for the phrase 'in session'.

B   Questions on 'The Houses of Parliament'

1   Where are the Houses of Parliament to be found?
2   What is another name for them?
3   When were the present Houses of Parliament built and why?
4   What are the two Chambers in Parliament and what is the major difference between them?
5   Why is the House of Commons still sometimes known as St Stephen's Chapel?
6   What is the present role of Mr Speaker and what was it in the past?
7   Where do visitors to the House of Commons sit?
8   What is the terrace sometimes used for by Members?
9   When is Parliament actually in session?
10   What signs are there which indicate when Parliament is sitting?

C   Grammar

1   Give the past tense, past participle, and present participle of these verbs.

creep, go, stand, haul, burn, feel, bring, become

2   Supply the correct preposition in the following sentences.

    a The M.P. spoke . . . . the subject in the debate.

    b The visitor handed his card . . . . the policeman.

    c The House of Commons is rich . . . . traditions.

    d Many Members abstained . . . . voting.

    e My M.P. is an expert . . . . foreign affairs.

    f An M.P. should try to make himself available . . . . his constituents.

    g A light was burning . . . . the face of Big Ben.

3   Supply the correct past tense of the verbs in brackets.

    a They . . . . (leave) the House after they . . . . (finish) their work.

    b By the time we . . . . (arrive) the debate . . . . (end).

    c He told me he . . . . (leave) the following morning.

    d I . . . . (discover) that my M.P. . . . . . (be) in the House of Commons for ten years.

    e I . . . . (be) not ready when he . . . . (tell) me it was time to go.

D   Explain the difference between the following pairs of similarly pronounced words.

hare/hair, heard/herd, find/fined, maid/made, hope/hop, scene/seen, teas/tease, sheep/ship, deep/dip

E   Write a brief account of the 'Houses of Parliament' in your own country.

English food

English food has a bad reputation abroad. This is most probably because foreigners in England are often obliged to eat in the more 'popular' type of restaurant. Here it is necessary to prepare food rapidly in large quantities, and the taste of the food inevitably suffers, though its quality, from the point of view of nourishment, is quite satisfactory. Still, it is rather dull and not always attractively presented. Moreover, the Englishman eating in a cheap or medium price restaurant is usually in a hurry—at least at lunch—and a meal eaten in a leisurely manner in pleasant surroundings is always far more enjoyable than a meal taken hastily in a business-like atmosphere. In general, it is possible to get an adequate meal at a reasonable price; in fact, such a meal may be less expensive than similar food abroad. For those with money to spare, there are restaurants that compare favourably with the best in any country.

In many countries breakfast is a snack rather than a meal, but the traditional English breakfast is a full meal. Some people have a cereal or porridge to begin with. If porridge is prepared from coarse oatmeal (in the proper Scottish manner) it is a tasty, economical, and nourishing dish, especially when it is eaten with milk or cream, and sugar or salt. Then comes a substantial, usually cooked, course such as bacon and eggs, sausages and bacon or, sometimes, haddock or kippers. Yorkshire ham is also a breakfast speciality. Afterwards comes toast, with butter and marmalade, and perhaps some fruit. Tea or coffee is drunk with the meal. Many English people now take such a full breakfast only on Sunday morning.

The traditional English meal (lunch or dinner, lunch generally being the lighter meal) is based on plain, simply-cooked food. British beefsteak is unsurpassed (with the best steaks coming from the Scotch Angus cattle) and is accompanied by roast potatoes, or potatoes done in their jackets; a second vegetable (probably cabbage or carrots), and Yorkshire pudding (baked batter, a mixture of flour, egg, milk and salt).

English lamb chops, best when grilled, make a very tasty dish, particularly when eaten with fresh spring peas, new potatoes and mint sauce. English pork is good, but English veal is sometimes disappointing.

As regards fish, Dover soles are a delicacy. So are British trout and salmon. Unfortunately, they are not cheap!

Take-away fish and chip shops sometimes sell other food, such as sausages and even curry.

Apple pie is a favourite sweet, and English puddings, of which there are various types, are an excellent ending to a meal, especially in winter.

English cheeses deserve to be better known than they are. The 'king' of cheeses is Stilton, a blue-veined cheese both smooth and strong, and at its best when port is drunk with it. Cheddar, Cheshire, and Lancashire cheeses are all pleasing to the palate, and cream cheeses are to be had in various parts of the country. In Devon, excellent clotted cream is made, which goes well with English strawberries and raspberries.

But what, you may say, shall we drink with our meal? Many will agree with the writer in answering: English beer, preferably bitter or pale ale, or cider. If it is real Devonshire country cider, be careful —it is stronger than you think when you first taste it!

In recent years the British have become more cosmopolitan in their eating habits, and many families frequently sit down to meals whose ingredients or recipes may come from India (curry is a well-liked dish), China, or indeed anywhere in the world.

Cheddar cheese goes well with fresh bread, pickled onions
and a tankard of beer.

A Vocabulary

1 Give the meaning of the following.
It has a bad reputation, with money to spare, it is unsurpassed,
pleasing to the palate
2 Give synonyms for the following words, or their meaning.
a It is a *dull* day.
b His speech was rather *dull*.
c The poor boy is rather *dull*; he'll never go far.
d I am *obliged* to leave today.
e I'm much *obliged* for your help.
f Tom was wearing a brown *jacket*.
g I liked potatoes baked in their *jackets*.
h You can easily see the *veins* on the back of the hands.
i How do they make the *veins* in that cheese?
3 Explain what is meant by the following.
mint (as in 'mint sauce'), inevitably, nourishment (as used in the
text, paragraph one), hastily, clotted

B Questions on 'English food'.

1 Why has English food a poor reputation abroad?
2 In what circumstances does one enjoy a meal most?
3 What sort of a meal is the traditional English breakfast?
4 What is characteristic of English food?
5 What is Yorkshire pudding?
6 With what is English lamb generally eaten?
7 What is Stilton?
8 With what English fruit does cream go well?
9 What should one drink with English food?

C Grammar

1 Complete the following sentences.
   a The fact that . . . . made me fall asleep.
   b The idea that . . . . was once widespread.
   c The principle that . . . . is democratic.
   d The suggestion that . . . . made me angry.
2 Insert the missing prepositions in the gaps in the following sentences.
   a . . . . my point . . . . view that is an advantage.
   b My theory is based . . . . various experiments.
   c This is the end . . . . the story.
   d It makes a good ending . . . . the story.
   e I agree . . . . you.
   f Tom was accompanied . . . . a friend.
   g . . . . Monday morning I got up early.

D Write an essay on: 'We should eat to live, and not live to eat'.

The weather

'Other countries have a climate; in England we have weather.' This statement, often made by Englishmen to describe the peculiar meteorological conditions of their country, is both revealing and true. It is revealing because in it we see the Englishman insisting once again that what happens in England is not the same as what happens elsewhere; its truth can be ascertained by any foreigner who stays in the country for longer than a few days.

In no country other than England, it has been said, can one experience four seasons in the course of a single day! Day may break as a balmy spring morning; an hour or so later black clouds may have appeared from nowhere and the rain may be pouring down. At midday conditions may be really wintry with the temperature down by about eight degrees or more centigrade. And then, in the late afternoon the sky will clear, the sun will begin to shine, and for an hour or two before darkness falls, it will be summer.

But we do have some sunny days!

In England one can experience almost every kind of weather except the most extreme. (Some foreigners, incidentally, seem to be under the impression that for ten months of the year the country is covered by a dense blanket of fog; this is not true.) The snag is that we never can be sure when the different types of weather will occur. Not only do we get several different sorts of weather in one day, but we may very well get a spell of winter in summer and vice-versa.

This uncertainty about the weather has had a definite effect upon the Englishman's character; it tends to make him cautious, for example. The foreigner may laugh when he sees the Englishman setting forth on a brilliantly sunny morning wearing a raincoat and carrying an umbrella, but he may well regret his laughter later in the day! The English weather has also helped to make the Englishman adaptable. It has been said that one of the reasons why the English colonized so much of the world was that, whatever the weather conditions they met abroad, they had already experienced something like them at home!

And, of course, the weather's variety provides a constant topic of conversation. Even the most taciturn of Englishmen is always prepared to discuss the weather. And, though he sometimes complains bitterly of it, he would not, even if he could, exchange it for the more predictable *climate* of other lands.

Thatched cottages look pretty in the snow.

A Vocabulary

1 What is the difference between the words *climate* and *weather?*
2 What is to *ascertain* the truth?
3 What does *balmy* mean?
4 What is meant by 'the *extreme* kinds of weather'?
5 Find another word for *dense* in the phrase 'dense blanket of fog'.
6 What does *to appear from nowhere* mean?
7 What is a *snag?*
8 What is a *spell* of winter? What is the other meaning of the word?
9 What are the countries called that are colonized? What are the inhabitants of those countries called?
10 Find a word or phrase meaning *taciturn.*
11 What does *predictable* mean? What is its opposite?

B Questions on 'The weather'

1 How would you distinguish the weather in England from that in many other countries?
2 How long do you think it would take you to discover the characteristics of English weather?
3 Describe briefly how you could experience 'four seasons in one day' in England.
4 What misapprehension are many foreigners under concerning Britain's weather?
5 What is the one constant characteristic of English weather?
6 How has the English weather affected the Englishman's character?
7 What connection, if any, do you think there may perhaps be between English weather and the growth of the British Empire?
8 Why is the weather a constant topic of conversation in England?
9 What is the Englishman's fundamental attitude towards his weather?

C   Grammar

1   Re-write the following sentences in reported speech.
   a I shall see you tomorrow.
   b Do you go to the cinema often?
   c If I were in your place I should think myself lucky!
   d We went there yesterday to see a good friend of ours.
   e Go home at once!
2   Put the verbs in the following sentences into their correct form.
   a I . . . . (go) home early because my mother . . . . (be) ill.
   b Whenever I . . . . (have) the chance, I . . . . (like) . . . .
   (go) into the country.
   c I . . . . (just leave) the office when I suddenly . . . .
   (bump) into an old friend of mine.
   d If I . . . . (be) careful I . . . . (prevent) many accidents.
   e I . . . . (accept) your advice even if it . . . . (mean) that
   I . . . . (have) . . . . (do) what I . . . . (dislike).

D   Put the following phrases into a sentence.

around the corner, from time to time, on the other side of,
as soon as possible, by the end of the week

E   Write an essay on the kind of weather you like best, giving
your reasons.

The seaside

No town in Britain is more than eighty miles from the sea and there are seaside resorts all round the coast. On a summer Sunday most of the roads that lead to the sea are congested with cars full of people eager to get a breath of sea air. Once at the beaches, the children hasten to unload their buckets and spades and start to build sandcastles or paddle in the shallow water. Father may go for a swim or sit and doze in his deck-chair while mother reads. In the evening when everyone is full of food, ice-cream and rock (a hard sweet in the form of a long stick), there is the long, slow drive home on roads crowded with returning cars.

The south coast is Britain's warmest and sunniest region. Along the whole coastline from Dover to Land's End are seaside towns with hotels and boarding houses, piers and promenades, cafés and restaurants, all catering for the thousands of visitors and holiday-makers. Brighton is one of the best-known south coast resorts and is very popular for day-trip excursions. It is only fifty miles from London and can be reached by fast train in an hour. At the week-end the pebbled beaches are thronged with people sun-bathing or picking their way to the water's edge for a dip. And always, at the end of the pier, there are a few hopeful people fishing.

At Bournemouth (in Dorset), which is a hundred miles from London, the beaches are wide and sandy. White houses line the

Children building a sandcastle

cliff tops and narrow chines (deep, narrow ravines), densely wooded with pine trees, reach down to the shore. The area near to the town of Torquay, on the Devon coast, is sometimes called Britain's Riviera and the climate is so mild that palm trees grow along the sea front.

Blackpool, on the north-west coast, is a popular resort for the people in the industrial north. Blackpool is a gay, noisy town, famous for its fun-fair and the illuminations. At night people travel from miles around to see the extravaganza of lights decorating the sea front.

Southend, on the east coast at the mouth of the Thames, is, like Brighton, a favourite resort of Londoners, particularly those from the East End. The sea shore is mainly grey mud, but this does not deter the crowds who come by train, car and Thames pleasure-steamer to enjoy themselves on Southend's front and mile-long pier. The pier is the longest in Britain and offers a great variety of differing entertainments.

These, then, are a very few of the holiday resorts scattered along Britain's coastline. For most Britons 'holiday' and 'seaside holiday' mean one and the same thing and, in the last fifty years or so, 'resorts' of every kind have sprung up to cater to the Englishman's need to spend a part of the year, however briefly, by the seaside. Of course, many British people go abroad for their holidays, and package tours to warmer countries are very popular with those who can afford them.

A   Vocabulary

1   What is the difference between a *hotel* and a *boarding house*?
2   One finds two kinds of rock at the seaside. Can you distinguish between the two?
3   What is the difference between a *pebbly* beach and a *rocky* beach?
4   The following are all things associated with the seaside. Can you define them?
speedboat, jellyfish, breakwater, bathing hut, sand-dune, seaweed, raft, seagull, life-guard, crab
5   Distinguish between a *pier* and a *promenade*.

6   What is a *paddle*?
7   What is a *dip*?
8   Give alternatives for the following words in the passage.
congested, densely wooded, *deter, sprung up*

B   Questions on 'The seaside'

1   Why do people pick their way to the water's edge at
Brighton?
2   What kind of trees are there growing near Bournemouth?
3   Why is the area near Torquay sometimes called Britain's
Riviera?
4   Where is Blackpool?
5   What is Blackpool famous for?
6   How long is the pier at Southend?
7   How do people get to the seaside?
8   Why do they often have a long, slow journey home?
9   Name two popular resorts for Londoners.
10   What does father like to do at the seaside?
11   What is the difference between the beach at Brighton and
the beach at Bournemouth?

C   Grammar

1   Insert the correct prepositions in the following sentences.
   a We stayed . . . . a bungalow . . . . the coast . . . . a week.
   b As we had no cups, we drank . . . . the bottle.
   c The air . . . . the seaside is very invigorating.
2   Give the comparative and superlative of these adjectives.
good, bad, old, much, short, little, merry, far
3   Fill in 'which', 'who', 'whom', or 'that' in the following
sentences. If the pronoun may be omitted, put it in brackets.
   a My friend, ... came with us, enjoyed himself very much.
   b Is this the man to . . . . you paid your money?
   c Where is the book . . . . I lent you yesterday?
   d All . . . . I use is a pair of scissors.
   e There is the man . . . . , I think, gave you the tomatoes.

D   Explain the following common idioms.

to see eye to eye with someone, to put one's foot in it, to pull someone's leg, to be well-off, to be hard-up, to get on like a house on fire

E   Form abstract nouns from these adjectives.

wise, poor, young, brave, proud, wide, great, hot

F   Write an essay on the pleasures of a seaside holiday or on the attraction of the sea.

Christmas

The Christmas tree in Trafalgar Square

In England, Christmas is the most important of all the 'Bank Holidays' in the year. Two important things, apart from its religious significance, help to set this holiday apart from all others: the custom of giving gifts and the habit of spending it with the family.

In the present highly commercialised age we are reminded of Christmas many weeks before the event. In the shops the special Christmas displays appear and outside them the special Christmas decorations. In the shopping centres of very large towns decorations are put up in the streets. In London thousands of people flock into the centre of the town to see the decorations in Oxford Street, Regent Street, Piccadilly and elsewhere. The advertisements in all the newspapers remind us incessantly that there are 'Only x more shopping days to Christmas'. The Post Office vans are covered with brightly coloured posters exhorting us to 'Post Early for Christmas', for hundreds of millions of Christmas cards and millions of parcels are sent every year. Everywhere one turns, one is made aware that Christmas, which comes 'but once a year', is coming once again.

Many people deplore what they consider the over-commercial-isation of a sacred holiday, but, underneath all the business activity,

Sorting parcels at the Post Office

a great deal of genuine Christmas spirit is to be found. The custom of giving presents to one's family and friends is a very pleasant one so long as one remembers that it is the spirit behind the gift which matters most and not the gift itself. And how good it is at Christmas to return to the family home and meet parents, grandparents and as many aunts, uncles and cousins as can be accommodated. Without twentieth-century means of transport, many families would be denied the Christmas reunion.

On Christmas Eve, the traditional ritual of hanging up a stocking at the foot of the bed is performed by millions of excited children. During the day the Christmas tree will have been dressed. All is now ready for the great morning, which comes round soon enough, in spite of the efforts of many of the younger children to stay awake until Santa Claus (or Father Christmas, as some call him) steals in to deliver the presents they have asked him for.

Christmas Day is spent quietly at home. The excitement of all the presents is hardly over before it is time for the traditional Christmas dinner: turkey, duck or chicken with rich fruity Christmas pudding afterwards. At tea-time the crackers are pulled. The evening is spent in games, merriment and more eating and drinking. There is always Boxing Day (the Bank Holiday after Christmas Day) on which to recover, if all the excitement and food have proved a little too much.

A   Vocabulary

1   What is a *Bank Holiday*?
2   Find an alternative for the expression *to set apart*.
3   Give a synonym for *gift*.
4   What do we do when we *display* something?
5   What word does the expression *to commercialise* come from?
6   The word *flock* is also used as a noun. Explain the meaning of both verb and noun.
7   What is an *advertisement*? What is the verb?
8   What does *to steal* mean in the phrase 'Santa Claus steals in'? The word has another more usual meaning. What is it?
9   What is a *custom*?
10   Explain the meaning of *ritual*.

11   What is a *pudding*?

12   Find a synonym for *merriment*.

B   Questions on 'Christmas'

1   What are the two important things which set the Christmas holiday apart from others?

2   In what ways do the shops remind us that Christmas is coming?

3   What happens to the streets of the larger town centres near Christmas time?

4   In what way does the Post Office remind us that Christmas is coming?

5   Why does the Post Office do this?

6   What is the attitude of some people toward all the commercial activity at Christmas time?

7   In what way do some twentieth century inventions help to preserve the Christmas spirit?

8   What traditional ritual is performed by the children on Christmas Eve?

9   How is Christmas Day spent?

10   What is Boxing Day useful for?

C   Grammar

1   Put the appropriate verbs in the following sentences into the passive voice.

    a On Christmas Day we always eat Christmas pudding.

    b On Christmas Eve we dress the tree and put stockings at the foot of our bed.

    c We are preparing the Christmas dinner.

    d The little boy loved his presents dearly.

    e We were pulling the crackers when our friends arrived.

    f Uncle Charlie will now sing a comic song.

    g We should remember those less fortunate than ourselves.

    h On Christmas Eve the postman delivered thirty Christmas cards.

2 In the following sentences replace the clause with *unless* by one with *if*.

   a I shall not go unless you come with me.
   b Unless you telephone to tell me not to, I will call tomorrow.
   c You will never succeed unless you try really hard.
   d I will never see you again unless you apologise.
   e He will never know, unless you tell him.

D Complete the following comparisons.

   1 He jumped from his seat as though . . . .
   2 The sudden news came to me like . . . .
   3 The bottle was empty and as dry as . . . .
   4 The soldier was as brave as . . . .
   5 The sea was as flat as . . . .
   6 The policeman pounced on the criminal like . . . .

E Write an essay describing any religious festival in your native country.

Guy Fawkes night

When November 5th comes, many people feel that they should give their dog a sedative, for some dogs get very nervous when they hear loud bangs, and the evening of Guy Fawkes Day is sure to be noisy if there are children living in your neighbourhood in England.

November 5th is a day on which, traditionally, children are allowed, under proper supervision, to let off fireworks, to make a bonfire and burn on it the figure of a ragged dummy (a 'guy') made of old clothes, straw, and—if possible—one of father's oldest hats. Even the smaller children are allowed to stay up until it is really dark, so that they can admire the rockets that burst in the sky and send down a shower of many-coloured sparks.

In the days before Guy Fawkes Day, some children may be seen going about the streets with their faces blackened, and wearing some kind of disguise. Sometimes they have a little cart or an old pram, and in it there is a 'guy'; they ask the passers-by to spare 'a penny for the guy'. With the coppers they get, they buy fireworks.

'A penny for the guy'.

The origin of this custom lies in the Gunpowder Plot of 1605. In that year King James I was on the throne. Harsh measures had been taken against members of the Roman Catholic faith and certain Catholics plotted to blow up the Houses of Parliament on November 5th, when the King was to open Parliament and when, of course, all the Members would be present. The plotters had hired premises adjoining the House of Lords, and had been able to obtain access to a vault beneath the House. There, they had stored thirty-six barrels of gunpowder. These were to be blown up, when the time came, by a very brave, cool-headed man, Guy Fawkes. Unfortunately, according to the traditional account, the plot was discovered when one of the plotters wrote to warn a relation. On November 4th the vaults were searched, and Guy Fawkes was found and arrested. It is said that he had been warned that the plot had been discovered, but he gallantly persisted in his purpose, hoping against hope that he might be favoured by chance and be able to rid his country of men whom he considered evil. He

Guy Fawkes, a print (1841) by George Cruikshank

was condemned to be hanged, along with others of his fellow-conspirators. He met his death with great fortitude.

It is the failure of this man, who was staunch in his faith though perhaps misguided in actions, that is perpetuated by the children's fireworks of November 5th. It is a poor tribute to Fawkes's courage that his Christian name, Guy, was long used in English to denote a person who is a figure of fun chiefly because of his odd dress.

A   Vocabulary

1   What effect does a *sedative* have on a person?
2   Give a synonym for a *plotter*.
3   Give an antonym for *noisy* and for *harsh*.
4   Give the meaning of the following words.
fireworks, a pram, bonfire, coppers, a rag, a throne, adjoining, straw, anonymous, to stay up, staunch, a disguise, faith
5   What would you do, if you were caught in a *shower*? In what room in a house would you expect to find a *shower*?
6   When two live electric wires touch, what do they produce?
7   What is the meaning of *spare* in 'Spare a penny for the guy'?
8   What is meant by 'to obtain access to'?
9   What is usually kept in *barrels*?
10   Where do we most frequently find a *vault*?
11   What is *gunpowder* used for?
12   What is meant by 'hoping against hope'?
13   What is the sense of *mis* in *misguided*?

B   Questions on 'Guy Fawkes night'

1   What may a dog be given on November 5th?
2   Name something that may make an animal nervous.
3   What are children allowed to do on Guy Fawkes Night?
4   What do some children do a little before Guy Fawkes Night?
5   Why did the plotters want to blow up the King and Parliament?
6   Where did they store the gunpowder?
7   Why was Guy Fawkes discovered?

8 What sort of a man was Guy Fawkes?
9 What was the fate of the plotters?
10 What has the word 'guy' come to mean?

C Grammar

1 Give the past simple and the present and past participles
of the verbs to *rid, burst,* and *burn*. What is the difference in usage
between the verbs 'hang, hung, hung' and 'hang, hanged,
hanged'?
2 Insert the correct preposition in each blank space where a
preposition is needed (otherwise insert no preposition).

a The manager left . . . . Leeds, where he had urgent
business.
b The clerk left . . . . his office when his work was done.
c Soldiers went . . . . the vault where the gunpowder was
hidden.
d They came down some steps and entered . . . . the vault.
e I entered . . . . conversation with a fellow passenger.
f I reminded him . . . . what was to be done.
g You should persist . . . . your efforts to learn English.
h My friend insisted . . . . paying for the meal.
i We must all learn to resist . . . . temptation.
j Was someone a traitor . . . . the plotters' cause?
k The figure was made . . . . straw.
l The children blacken their faces . . . . soot.
m The rocket shot up . . . . a cloud.
n Guy Fawkes was surrounded . . . . the King's soldiers.
o The King had been warned . . . . the plot.

D Tell the story of a historical plot in your own country or the
story of some famous man of your own country.

The Highway Code

Every year in Britain, nearly six thousand people are killed on the roads. Although the percentage of casualties is not as large as in some other countries, the Government is seriously worried by this problem. They fear that with the increasing number of vehicles coming on to the roads each year the total number of casualties will also continue to grow. One of the greatest problems in Britain is the lack of space. It is extremely difficult, especially in the cities, to obtain any extra land in order to improve existing roads and the acquiring of sufficient land on which to build new roads often seems nearly impossible.

In spite of all the difficulties, however, improvements are being made, although motorists (and pedestrians too) are still not satisfied with the rate of progress, particularly when they think of the taxes they have to pay!

It remains true, however, that the standards of safety on the roads will not be improved simply by improving the roads. The attitude of the users of the road is the most important factor in improving road safety. This is why the government and local authorities devote time and resources to producing 'propaganda' in support of the 'Safety First' campaign which is constantly being waged. Posters, broadcasts on the radio, special 'Safety First' weeks are some of the means employed.

Perhaps the best-known piece of 'propaganda' for safety on the road is the government's booklet *The Highway Code*. This costs only a few pence and gives, with illustrations, all the rules and conventions in use on the roads of Britain. The fundamental convention of road usage in Britain (and one that usually gives foreigners a pleasant surprise) is that the pedestrian has 'the right of way'. That is to say, the pedestrian is assumed to have priority in road usage. The sense of this rule is apparent when one considers that a pedestrian is not in a position to injure a driver whereas the reverse is certainly true. Every foreigner who intends to drive in Britain should obtain a copy of the code and read it carefully.

It is probably true to say that the British motorists are as careful as most others in the world. (The same is not, perhaps, true of the pedestrians, who are rather spoiled.) Even so, their standards must be raised considerably higher if the country is to succeed in its attempt (in the words of an early safety-first poster) to 'Keep Death off the Road'.

Top Some signs from *The Highway Code*
Bottom Motorways meet at 'Spaghetti Junction'.

A   Vocabulary

1   What is a *casualty*?
2   Define *total*.
3   What is the opposite of *difficult*?
4   Find a synonym for *to acquire*.
5   What is a *pedestrian*?
6   Explain the phrase 'the rate of progress'.
7   What do you do when you *improve* something?
8   What are *local authorities*?
9   What does *resources* mean in 'time and resources'?
10   Find a synonym for *constantly*.
11   What is a *booklet*? Give another word of the same meaning.
12   What is the difference between a *rule* and a *convention*?
13   What is the *reverse* of something?

B   Questions on 'The Highway Code'

1   What effect has the number of road casualties every year had upon the Government?
2   What does the Government fear will happen to the total number of casualties?
3   What particular problem is Britain faced with in trying to improve roads?
4   What is the most important factor in improving road safety?
5   Name at least two ways in which local authorities try to make people safety conscious.
6   What is the best-known piece of 'propaganda' on road safety?
7   State what the Highway Code contains.
8   Why is the pedestrian assumed to have priority on English roads?
9   What would be your advice to a foreigner intending to drive on English roads?
10   What must happen before conditions on English roads become appreciably safer?

C   Grammar

1   Insert *yet* or *still* as needed in the following sentences.
    a 'Has our visitor arrived . . . . ?' 'No, not . . . . '
    b I . . . . do not know the answer to that question.
    c I . . . . haven't heard from him, so I can't say . . . .
    whether he will come or not.
    d Is it . . . . raining?
    e I'm not . . . . ready, but I shall be soon.
    f Mary has been in the bathroom an hour and she is . . . .
    not ready.
2   Insert the missing prepositions in the following sentences.
    a The booklet is recommended . . . . all road users.
    b Pedestrians should be on guard . . . . careless drivers.
    c Drivers should give priority . . . . pedestrians.
    d He was criticized . . . . the policeman for his bad driving.
    e One should always keep . . . . the correct side of the road.

D   Complete the verbal expressions in the following sentences.

1   I must tidy up sometime, but I keep putting it . . . .
2   How can you put . . . . his dreadful behaviour?
3   'Put . . . . your toys before you go to bed,' said mother.
4   'Put . . . . your tongue,' said the doctor.
5   I often put my friend . . . . when he visits town.
6   It is my job to put the cat . . . . every night.
7   Put . . . . your hand if you know the answer.
8   One should always try to put . . . . a little money in case of
emergency.

E   Write an essay on 'The Traffic Problem'.

The Welfare State

Every British citizen who is employed (or self-employed) is obliged to pay a weekly contribution to the national insurance and health schemes. An employer also makes a contribution for each of his employees, and the Government too pays a certain amount. This plan was brought into being in 1948. Its aim is to prevent anyone from going without medical services, if he needs them, however poor he may be; to ensure that a person who is out of work shall receive a weekly sum of money to subsist on; and to provide a small pension for those who have reached the age of retirement.

Everyone can register with a doctor of his choice and if he is ill he can consult the doctor without having to pay for the doctor's services, although he has to pay a small charge for medicines. The doctor may, if necessary, send a patient to a specialist, or to a

An operation in progress

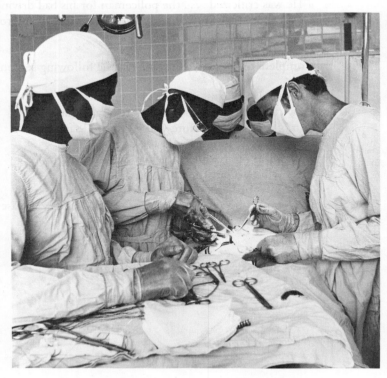

hospital; in both cases treatment will be given without any fee being payable. Those who wish may become private patients, paying for their treatment, but they must still pay their contributions to the national insurance and health schemes.

During illness the patient can draw a small amount every week, to make up for his lost wages. Everyone who needs to have his eyes seen to may go to a state-registered oculist and if his sight is weak he can get spectacles from an optician at a much reduced price. For a small payment he may go to a dentist; if he needs false teeth, he can obtain dentures for less than they would cost from a private dentist. Various other medical appliances can be obtained in much the same way.

When a man is out of work, he may draw unemployment benefit until he finds work again; this he will probably do by going to a Job Centre (an office run by the State to help people find jobs). If he is married, the allowance he receives will be larger. Obviously, the amount paid is comparatively small, for the State does not want people to stop working in order to draw a handsome sum of money for doing nothing!

When a man reaches the age of sixty-five, he may retire from work and then he has the right to draw a State pension. For women, the age of retirement is sixty.

Mothers-to-be and children receive special benefits such as free milk or certain foodstuffs for which only a minimum charge is made. The State pays to the mother a small weekly sum for each child in a family. There is also an allowance for funerals, for the State boasts that it looks after people 'from the cradle to the grave'! There are special benefits for certain people, such as the blind and the handicapped.

The amount of money needed to operate these schemes is enormous and a large part of the money comes not from the contributions but from taxation.

Most people in Britain agree that there are still many improvements to be made in our national insurance and health schemes, but it is also true that they have become a social institution that the great majority of the population wishes to see maintained.

It is this social insurance scheme, together with the Government's determination to see that there is full employment (or as near as can be), that constitutes what we call the 'Welfare State'.

A Vocabulary

1 Explain the meaning of the following words or phrases.
self-employed, a fee, to bring into being, to boast, to subsist,
a cradle, retirement, a grave, grave (adjective)
2 Explain the meaning of *obliged* in the following sentences.
   a The bandits obliged the travellers to dismount.
   b I am much obliged to you for your help.
3 What is the difference between the business terms *insurance*
and *assurance*?
4 Find in the text another word for *amount*.
5 What verb corresponds to the noun *choice*?
6 Explain the difference between an *oculist* and an *optician*.
7 Give the opposites of *minimum* and *majority*.
8 Explain the meanings of *to draw* in the following sentences.
   a The artist drew something on the paper.
   b The cart was drawn by a horse.
   c You may draw on a special account for expenses.
   d The cowboy drew his revolver.
   e From an early age he was drawn to crime.

B Questions on 'The Welfare State'

1 To what welfare schemes must an employed British citizen
contribute?
2 Who else must also contribute?
3 What is the purpose of these contributions?
4 Does a patient have to pay a State-registered doctor a fee?
5 What is the advantage of getting such things as spectacles
through the National Health Service?
6 Why doesn't the State pay an unemployed man a large
unemployment benefit?
7 At what age do men generally retire?
8 Are the contributions to the social service schemes enough
to pay for them?
9 What is the attitude of most people in Britain to social
insurance?
10 What is meant by the term 'Welfare State'?

C   Grammar

1   Give the past simple and the past and present participles of these verbs.

to draw, lose, agree, employ, receive

2   Insert *whatever, however, whoever, whenever* or *wherever* as needed.

    a . . . . fast you run you will never catch up with Bill!

    b . . . . told you such a ridiculous story?

    c I will go there with you . . . . you like.

    d Tom's bulldog follows him . . . . he goes.

    e . . . . he is in trouble he says a prayer.

    f . . . . have you been doing? Your face is black!

    g . . . . can this curious thing be?

    h . . . . can have sent me such a lovely present?

    i . . . . can I have put my spectacles?

    j . . . . shall I do? I've lost my purse.

3   State in which of the following sentences the surgeon is the more pessimistic.

    a Well, the patient may survive such an operation.

    b Well, the patient might survive such an operation.

4   Insert *may, might, can, could,* or *been able to* as needed.

    a Oh dear, what . . . . the matter be? My watch won't go.

    b There are some clouds about: it . . . . rain this afternoon.

    c No, Willie, you . . . . not smoke in class.

    d Have you . . . . find someone to do the job for you?

    e We were told that we . . . . use dictionaries for this test.

    f He told me that he . . . . mend the set as he was an expert.

    g Please . . . . I open the window?

    h I . . . . hear what you are saying; there's no need to shout!

    i I told him he . . . . hurt himself badly if he did that.

    j When I was young I . . . . run very fast.

D   Write an essay on one of the following subjects.

    a Social insurance in your own country

    b A doctor's waiting room

    c At the dentist's

The schools

In recent years the educational system for England and Wales (Scotland has its own system) has been re-organised. In 1972, the school-leaving age was raised from fifteen to sixteen, so now all children have a minimum of eleven years compulsory full-time education. Children begin their education in the State system at the age of five; some lucky ones may have the opportunity to attend one of the few Nursery Schools from the age of three to five, but most children start their basic education in an Infants' or First School. At seven or eight they move on to the next stage.

A few years ago the most commonly found arrangement of schools in any district was that of Primary Schools (including Infants) for children up to the age of eleven, and then Secondary Schools for children over eleven. Nowadays there are a number of different systems in operation; some areas still retain the Primary Schools with the change-over to secondary education at eleven, but many Local Education Authorities (which are autonomous bodies) have created Middle Schools for children aged eight to twelve and these pupils transfer to Comprehensive Secondary Schools when they are nearly thirteen. These Comprehensive Schools take children of all abilities from the neighbourhood, and as well as a general education, these schools offer a wide range of academic courses leading to the public examinations taken at

Children making a picture in a Primary School

sixteen, and some handicraft and vocationally orientated courses.

There are very few local education areas where children are still selected for secondary education by means of an examination (which was known as the 'eleven plus'), and almost all of the former 'Grammar Schools' have been absorbed into the Comprehensive Schools. Some of the older Grammar Schools, however, have withdrawn from the State system and have become private schools, charging fees and choosing their pupils by entrance examinations. This independent sector of education (which includes the well-known 'Public schools' as well as other privately endowed schools) provides for the education of about six per cent of the school population.

Any child may leave school at sixteen without attempting any of the public examinations, but an increasing number of boys and girls are taking the Certificate of Secondary Education examinations or the General Certificate of Education. Both the CSE and the GCE are 'public' examinations conducted by examining Boards and standardised to give national comparability. The GCE is intended for pupils of an academic bias and (theoretically) any number of subjects may be taken. The CSE, like the GCE, has a subject range covering all of those likely to be taught in school. It is, however, designed for those pupils who are less academically

A modern Secondary School

able. A pupil may take GCE in some subjects and CSE in others.

A large proportion of the children taking a group of subjects at 'O' Level (an abbreviation used for the General Certificate of Education at Ordinary Level) will probably continue in full-time education and work for the GCE Advanced Level examinations. This they can do by staying on in the sixth form of their school, or by enrolling at a Sixth Form College or a College of Further Education. For those who want to go on into higher education the Advanced Level GCE examination is very important, for it is on the results of this examination that the universities and polytechnics choose their students.

A   Vocabulary

1   What is the opposite of these words?
compulsory, minimum, lucky, different, plus, general
2   Explain the meaning of *basic* in the phrase 'basic education'.
3   Why is a Comprehensive School so called?
4   What is a *certificate*?
5   What does *comparability* mean in the phrase 'standardised to give national comparability'?
6   What does to *attempt* normally mean? Find the correct synonym for it in the phrase 'without attempting any of the public examinations'?
7   What is an *entrance examination*?
8   Find a synonym for *nowadays*.

B   Questions on 'The schools'

1   Between what ages, in England and Wales, must every child attend school regularly?
2   What is another name for an Infants' School?
3   At what ages do children go on to Secondary School?
4   What was the 'eleven plus'?
5   What purpose are the results of the GCE 'Advanced' level examination used for?
6   What is the difference between the 'O' level GCE and CSE?

7 What are two important differences between private schools and State schools?

8 What important educational change took place in 1972?

9 What are 'Middle Schools'?

C Grammar

1 Insert the correct prepositions in the following sentences.
a My schooling began . . . . the age of five and continued for eleven years.
b Some people do not approve . . . . Comprehensive Schools.
c One must persevere . . . . one's education if one is eager . . . . success.
d It is everyone's duty to be concerned . . . . the kind of education that is being provided . . . . the country.
e It is interesting to compare the system of our country . . . . that of another; we may learn much . . . . doing so.

2 Put the following sentences into indirect speech beginning each one with 'He said that . . . . '
a I am not going to school next week because we are having a holiday.
b Tomorrow my cousin is coming home from his Public school.
c Many changes have been made in the educational system in recent years.
d If I pass my 'O' Levels, I should like to go to a Sixth Form College to work for my 'A' Levels.

D Explain clearly the meaning of the following proverbs.

Necessity is the mother of invention; More haste less speed; Once bitten twice shy; It never rains but it pours; A stitch in time saves nine; Too many cooks spoil the broth; Charity begins at home.

E Write an essay on 'A Good Education'.

Further education

The term 'Further Education' is the name given, in Britain, to a very broad and diverse range of post-school education. Some is full-time, some is part-time and some is half-and-half with periods at college alternating with periods at work. (These are called 'sandwich' courses). There is also a vast and varied provision of evening classes. For many older people, evening study was the only way they could pursue their education and they still think of the institution that provided it as 'Night School'.

Nowadays, however, the opportunities for Further Education at all levels and for all ages are manifold. The courses provided range from the most elementary, directly vocationally-orientated kind, to those at degree level or beyond. They are provided in a widely differing set of institutions. The majority of the lower level courses, relating mainly to apprenticeship schemes and qualifications, are provided in Colleges of Further Education or Technical Colleges. Middle level courses are also offered in Technical Colleges with those having a good share of more advanced work being called 'Colleges of Technology'. The great bulk of advanced studies and degree level work is undertaken in the Polytechnics. But there are a number of specialised colleges such as the London College of Printing and the National College of Agricultural Engineering. Very few of the broad divisions here are clear cut; there is much overlapping.

One of the major areas of 'overlap' that has occurred during the past ten years or so has been between the school system and Further Education. There has been a growing provision of 'Sixth Form' level studies in Colleges of Further Education and Technical Colleges during this period and almost all of the 'non-advanced' technical colleges now offer a broad spread of subjects for the GCE Advanced Level ('A' level) examinations. Many sixth form students seem to prefer the more adult atmosphere of the Technical College to that of the school. A few Local Education Authorities have decided, partly because of this existing trend and partly for reasons of economy, that all the post-sixteen education in certain areas— both technical and academic—should be amalgamated in one establishment; such amalgamated institutions are called 'Tertiary Colleges'.

Whatever the type of establishment and its range of educational provision, most of the local inhabitants will probably refer to it as

A training course for nurses

'the Tech'. The Tech has played an important part in British educational history and its role will be no less important in the future.

A   Vocabulary

1   Give a synonym for the adjective *diverse*. What is the verb?
2   What is a *trend*?
3   Explain the word *course* as used in the passage. Can you think of two other meanings of the same word?
4   Explain why a *sandwich course* is so called.
5   Find a synonym for *amalgamated*.

6 What is a *vocation*? What does the term mean in its strict sense?

7 Give three words that mean the opposite of *vast*.

B Questions on 'Further education'

1 What are the major characteristics of the Further Education system?

2 Why do older people associate Further Education with 'Night School'?

3 What methods of study, other than by full-time courses, are provided by the 'Techs'?

4 What sort of range do the courses in further education institutions cover?

5 Name two 'specialised' colleges. Why do you think such specialised colleges exist?

6 Why are some Local Education Authorities providing all post-sixteen education in Tertiary Colleges?

7 Why have many sixth form students been choosing to study in a Technical College?

C Grammar

Insert the appropriate relative pronoun in the following sentences (who, whom, whose; which, that). If the pronoun may be omitted, put it in brackets.

a The car .... I drive is ten years old.

b His story, ... happens to be true, sounds incredible.

c This is the boy .... pen I borrowed.

d He returned the money .... I lent him quite quickly, ... was very pleasant.

e Everything .... I do seems to be wrong.

f The gentleman to .... I have been speaking is a very good friend of mine.

g Our cat, ... is a very wild animal, likes to pull up the plants.

h The cat .... I saw in the garden last night was not ours.

D   Complete the following idiomatic comparisons.

. . . . as a needle, ... as a cucumber, ... as a door nail,
. . . . as lightning, ... as a March hare, ... as a lord,
. . . . as a judge, ... as a rock, ... as houses

E   Write an essay outlining what you know of the Further
Education system in your country.

Universities and polytechnics

The two best known universities in England are also the oldest seats of learning: Oxford and Cambridge. These two universities date back to the thirteenth century and they consist of a number of colleges founded and built, for the most part, in the early years of the Universities' existence. For both the resident students and the visitors, the Universities are collections of buildings of great historical interest.

It was not until the beginning of the nineteenth century that the creation of more universities was seen to be either necessary or desirable. One of the first new foundations was London University (1827) which, following the organisational structure of the ancient foundations, also consists of a number of constituent colleges. New provincial universities were established in the early part of the twentieth century—Sheffield (1905) and Bristol (1909) being among the first—and these set up a different pattern of university

The Meeting House, Sussex University

life. Most of the teaching and lecturing takes place in the main buildings of the university and the students live in hostels (known as Halls of Residence) or lodgings in the town.

In 1945 there were 17 universities in Britain; by 1967 there were 45. A period of very rapid expansion took place in the middle sixties when ten new institutions were granted university status by Royal Charter. These modern universities do not in many respects resemble their older counterparts. Much more emphasis is placed on advanced studies in science and technology and the newer social science disciplines than on the arts and humanities. For the most part the buildings the students live and work in are severely functional and there is the hum and bustle of continuous activity. The quiet gardens and enclosed quadrangles of Oxford and Cambridge belong to another world. This is inevitable, for the universities like everything else must change and adapt themselves to meet the needs and demands of a new age.

In recent years there has been a very rapid increase in the numbers of young people (especially girls) seeking higher education. Between 1962 and 1975, the number of students in higher education more than doubled from 222,400 to 497,000. Part of this increase is accounted for by the creation of thirty 'Polytechnics' which offer a wide range of courses leading to recognised qualifications. The polytechnics were created by amalgamating existing specialised colleges and Colleges of Advanced Technology into one institution; these new establishments undertake a considerable amount of work which is comparable in standard to that of the universities, and an increasing proportion of their students qualify for degrees validated by the Council for National Academic Awards (CNAA).

For those people who missed the opportunity for higher education at the age of eighteen or thereabouts, a major innovation in the academic world now provides a second chance. The Open University was founded in 1971; it offers tuition to degree standard to anyone who chooses to register—there are no formal academic qualifications required for entry. The courses are taught through radio and television programmes and by correspondence with Open University tutors. By 1976 there were more than 90,000 students enrolled for Open University courses and there are several thousand people who are the proud holders of a B.A. degree from the Open University.

A   Vocabulary

1   What is a *resident*?
2   What is another word for *student*—used particularly at Oxford and Cambridge?
3   Distinguish between *necessary* and *desirable*.
4   What is a *constituent* college?
5   What is the difference between *science* and *technology*?
6   What is the opposite of *expansion*?
7   Explain the phrase 'severely functional'.
8   Explain the difference between *find* and *found* (as used in the passage).
9   What is a Hall of Residence?

B   Questions on 'Universities and polytechnics'

1   What distinguishes Oxford and Cambridge from other English universities?
2   What major educational innovation occurred in 1971?
3   What was the increase in the number of universities in Britain between 1945 and 1967?
4   What is the difference between the ten universities created in the 1960s and their older counterparts?
5   Can people living in Britain who missed the chance of a university education early in life do anything about it?
6   How did the British educational system cope with the greatly increased demand for higher education between 1962 and 1975?
7   How old are Oxford and Cambridge Universities?
8   What distinguishes the Open University from all other British Universities?

C   Grammar

1   Put the following sentences into reported speech.
    a I shall have a great many books to buy when I go up to the university next week.

b When I was at university I spent too much time on the playing fields and not enough in the library.

c 'All work and no play makes Jack a dull boy', but the reverse is also true.

d How pleasant it is to be a young student and to know the answers to all the world's problems!

e Will you lend me your notes on yesterday's lectures?

f Let me take you on the river this afternoon; you can read while I row.

g Always try to keep work and play completely separate or all your time will be wasted.

h It is impossible for me to go out today, I have an examination tomorrow morning.

2 Insert the correct preposition in the following sentences.

a Attendance . . . . lectures is not compulsory.

b The key . . . . success is hard work, but not too much of it!

c He met . . . . an accident just before his final examination.

d When I first visited Oxford I was overwhelmed . . . . the beauty of the old buildings.

e I have the greatest respect . . . . my professor.

f At Cambridge I developed a taste . . . . Norman architecture.

g When I was at college I divided my time . . . . study and sport.

h I knew I could always confide . . . . my tutor if something was wrong.

i Fortunately I was successful . . . . all my examinations.

j He instilled a real love of learning . . . . me.

D Put each of the following idiomatic expressions into a sentence.

now and then, time after time, first and foremost, to and fro, once and for all, by and large, through and through, again and again

E Write an essay on 'The Ideal University'.

Shakespeare

Olivia Hussey in the film of *Romeo and Juliet*

For any Englishman, there can never be any discussion as to who is the world's greatest poet and greatest dramatist. Only one name can possibly suggest itself to him: that of William Shakespeare. Every Englishman has some knowledge, however slight, of the work of our greatest writer. All of us use words, phrases and quotations from Shakespeare's writings that have become part of the common property of English-speaking people. Most of the time we are probably unaware of the source of the words we use, rather like the old lady who was taken to see a performance of *Hamlet* and complained that 'it was full of well-known proverbs and quotations'!

Shakespeare, more perhaps than any other writer, made full use of the great resources of the English language. Most of us use about five thousand words in our normal employment of English; Shakespeare in his works used about twenty-five thousand! There is probably no better way for a foreigner (or an Englishman!) to appreciate the richness and variety of the English language than by studying the various ways in which Shakespeare uses it. Such a study is well worth the effort (it is not, of course, recommended to beginners), even though some aspects of English usage, and the meaning of many words, have changed since Shakespeare's day.

It is paradoxical that we should know comparatively little about the life of the greatest English author. We know that Shakespeare was born in 1564 in Stratford-on-Avon, and that he died there in 1616. He almost certainly attended the Grammar School in the town, but of this we cannot be sure. We know he was married there in 1582 to Anne Hathaway and that he had three children, a boy and two girls. We know that he spent much of his life in London writing his masterpieces. But this is almost all that we do know.

However, what is important about Shakespeare's life is not its incidental details but its products, the plays and the poems. For many years scholars have been trying to add a few facts about Shakespeare's life to the small number we already possess and for an equally long time critics have been theorising about the plays. Sometimes, indeed, it seems that the poetry of Shakespeare will disappear beneath the great mass of comment that has been written upon it.

Fortunately this is not likely to happen. Shakespeare's poetry and Shakespeare's people (Macbeth, Othello, Hamlet, Falstaff and all the others) have long delighted not just the English but lovers of literature everywhere, and will continue to do so after the scholars and commentators and all their works have been forgotten.

A Vocabulary

1 Find a synonym for the verb *to discuss*.
2 What is a *phrase*?
3 What is *common property*?
4 What is the meaning of the word *source* in the passage? Can you give another meaning of the word?
5 Find a synonym of *employment* in the phrase 'our normal employment of English'.
6 Can you distinguish between *richness* and *variety*?
7 What is the meaning of *paradoxical*?
8 What is the noun from which *theorising* is derived?
9 What are *incidental* details?
10 What is a *commentator*?

B   Questions on 'Shakespeare'

1   Name one of the things which all Englishmen possess in common.

2   Why did the old lady complain that *Hamlet* was 'full of well-known proverbs and quotations'?

3   What difference is there between the vocabulary of the average Englishman and that of Shakespeare's plays?

4   What has happened to some of the words that Shakespeare used?

5   What is rather paradoxical about the greatest English author?

6   Where did Shakespeare spend most of his life?

7   Where do we think Shakespeare was educated?

8   What have Shakespearian scholars been trying to do for many years?

9   All the theorising about Shakespeare's plays may have a bad effect. Why?

10   Whom do Shakespeare's creations delight?

C   Grammar

1   Insert a suitable interrogative pronoun or adjective in the following sentences.

    a .... is the man in the doorway?

    b .... brief case is this? Yours or mine?

    c .... do you prefer, tennis or cricket?

    d .... did you see at the meeting?

    e .... sort of cooking do you prefer, French or English?

    f .... does that soup taste like?

    g These balls all look alike; .... is .... ?

    h .... shall we do next?

2   Insert *but, in spite of, although (though)*, as needed, in the following sentences.

    a We went for a walk .... the rain.

    b We went for a walk .... it was raining.

    c He is brilliant .... erratic.

    d .... for my friends, I should be a very lonely man.

e He could not .... laugh .... the joke was against him.

f .... he was ill and .... his weakness, he worked on.

D   Explain the meaning of the following proverbs clearly in
a single sentence.

Too many cooks spoil the broth, A miss is as good as a mile,
A bird in the hand is worth two in the bush, Birds of a feather
flock together, Forewarned is forearmed

E   Write an essay on 'My Country's Greatest Author'.

Music in Britain

It is debatable whether the tastes of kings reflect those of their subjects. However, three English monarchs certainly shared their people's liking for music. Richard I (1157-1199), the 'Lionheart', composed songs that he sang with his minstrel, Blondel. It is said that when the king was a prisoner in Austria, Blondel found him by singing a song known only to him and the king, who took up the tune in the tower of the castle in which he was secretly imprisoned. Henry VIII (1491-1547), notorious for his six wives, was a skilled musician and some of his songs are still known and sung. Queen Victoria (1819-1901) and her husband, Prince Albert, delighted in singing ballads. The great composer and pianist Felix Mendel-

A concert in the Royal Festival Hall

ssohn (1809-1847) was a welcome guest at their court, where he would accompany the Queen and the Prince Consort when they sang. Mendelssohn had a great liking for Scotland, which is shown in his 'Scottish Symphony' and the overture 'The Hebrides'.

The British love of music is often unfamiliar to foreigners, probably because there are few renowned British composers. The most famous is Henry Purcell (1658-1695), whose opera 'Dido and Aeneas' is a classic. The rousing marching song 'Lillibulero' attributed to Purcell, now used by the BBC as an identification signal preceding Overseas Service news bulletins, was said to have 'sung James II out of three kingdoms' when he fled from Britain in 1688. Sir Edward Elgar (1857-1934) is known for his choral and orchestral works, some of which have been made more widely known by the famous violinist Yehudi Menuhin. Benjamin Britten (1913-1976), a composer with a very personal style, has become world-famous for such operatic works as 'Peter Grimes' and 'Billy Budd'. Ralph Vaughan Williams (1872-1958) was deeply influenced by English folk-music, as is shown by his variations on the old tune 'Greensleeves' (which most people consider a folk-song). In recent years there has been a great revival of folk-music, and groups specialising in its performance have sprung up all over Britain. This phenomenon has its roots in the work of Cecil Sharp (1859-1924), who collected folk songs and dances (in which both Vaughan Williams and Elgar took an active interest).

Present-day concern with music is shown by the existence of something like a hundred summer schools in music, which cater for all grades of musicians, from the mere beginner to the skilled performer. These schools, where a friendly atmosphere reigns, provide courses lasting from a week-end to three or four weeks, and cover a wide range, from medieval and classical music to rock-and-roll and pop. There are also important musical festivals in towns such as Aldeburgh, Bath, and Cheltenham. Pop-music festivals draw thousands of people, especially young people. In the great cities there are resident world-famous orchestras and from all over the world great performers come to play or sing in Britain. In many towns there are brass bands, and the players are often such people as miners or members of the local fire-brigade, for music in Britain is not just a highbrow interest, it is above all democratic.

Part of the Brass section at the London Schools Concert

A   Vocabulary

1   Give a synonym for *debatable* as used in, 'It is debatable
whether . . . .'. What is the verb from which the adjective *debatable*
is derived?
2   What is the difference between a *monarch* and a *king*?
3   Give a synonym for *lion-hearted*.
4   What is the difference between *notorious* and *famous*?
5   Give the opposite of *skilled*, using a prefix.
6   Make a sentence using the verb *to rouse* and another using
to arouse.
7   Give an opposite for *preceding*.
8   What is the meaning of *roots* in 'This phenomenon has its
roots in'?
9   Give a synonym for *mainly*.
10   What work does a *fire-brigade* do?
11   What is meant by *highbrow*?

B   Questions on 'Music in Britain'

1   Do monarchs and their subjects always have the same likes
and dislikes?
2   How did the imprisoned King Richard I make himself known
to the minstrel Blondel?
3   In what way did Mendelssohn *accompany* Queen Victoria and
Prince Albert?
4   Why do foreigners often think that the British are not
fond of music?
5   Was Mendelssohn influenced by the music of any particular
nation? If so, which?
6   Why is it possible to hear the song 'Lillibulero' all over the
world?
7   What shows that folk-music is now popular in Britain?
8   Is interest in music in Britain limited to any particular
kind of music?
9   Who might be especially fond of pop music?
10   What shows us that it is wrong to think that music in
Britain is only for intellectuals?

C Grammar

Insert the missing prepositions in the following sentences.
1 Some British kings had a taste . . . . music.
2 Most people think that the taste . . . . castor-oil is horrible.
3 Tommy, share your cake . . . . your little sister.
4 The secret was known . . . . two people only.
5 Benjamin Britten is known . . . . his operas.
6 Scotland is famous . . . . bagpipe music.
7 I take no interest . . . . that subject.
8 James II was chased out . . . . Britain.
9 The opera 'Dido and Aeneas' is familiar . . . . lovers of
17th century music.
10 The Queen entered, accompanied . . . . the Prince Consort.

D Write a short essay on 'The Sort of Music I Like'.

Agriculture in Britain

The visitor who travels from Dover to London in Spring will pass through blossoming orchards of apple, pear and cherry trees, for it is not for nothing that Kent is called the 'Garden of England'. Hard fruits (apples and pears) grow well in many other parts of Britain also, their worst enemy being a late frost. In the West, we find farmers devoting thousands of acres to the growing of cider apples (an acre is about four-tenths of a hectare). Soft fruits (such as plums, strawberries, blackcurrants) are grown in many counties; the area around Perth, in Scotland, is the chief centre for raspberries.

Although Britain is so densely populated (325 persons per square kilometre), agriculture is a most important industry. It gives employment to over six hundred thousand people, who produce about half the food requirements of the country. The high rate of production per hectare is due to generally fertile soil, a long tradition of good husbandry, and the extensive use of modern technical improvements. A variety of artificial fertilisers have been developed, and so too have many chemicals and sprays that enable the farmer to get rid of the pests that would otherwise diminish output. Government agricultural experts and research establishments provide advice and information. There is a high degree of mechanization, and Britain has one of the highest tractor densities

A combine harvester at work

in the world—there are now over half a million tractors in use, as
well as numerous harvesting machines. It is such developments as
these that allow our agriculture to produce more today than was
produced, with a greater labour force, before the war. Since joining
the European Economic Community in 1973, Britain has adopted
the Community system of agricultural support.

Wheat growing is confined mainly to England, with average
yields of 4.3 tonnes per hectare. New varieties of wheat have been
successfully introduced. Barley is grown extensively, either for
malting or as a food for livestock. Oats and turnips are grown in
appreciable but diminishing quantities.

Sugar beet is found in East Anglia and in Lincolnshire, and the
output is handled by the British Sugar Corporation. More than
half the crop is harvested mechanically. The cultivation of potatoes
is also highly mechanized; they are grown mainly in the East of
England, and in Lancashire, while Scotland supplies seed-raising
potatoes.

Dairy farming is distributed all over the country but is character-

Corn stacks from John Slezer's *Theatrum Scotiae*, 1693

istic of the West of England; the consumption of liquid (pasteur-ised) milk is high in Britain—an average of 2.75 litres a week per person (a good deal goes into the many cups of tea that people drink every day!). Tuberculosis in cows has been eradicated in most parts of the country.

Britain is the world's leading exporter of pedigree livestock: cattle, sheep, pigs, horses. Cattle are bred for meat (beefsteak) as well as for dairy farming. Sheep are found in hilly counties particu-larly and are bred chiefly for their meat. Hens' eggs of high quality are sold with the help of a national marketing board; chickens, for eating, are reared in huge numbers and are now very cheap.

Market gardening centres are usually situated near the big towns. Glasshouses are found mainly in southern England. The Channel Islands, Cornwall and the Scilly Isles are the greatest providers of early vegetables and flowers. A few vineyards are now providing Britain with home-grown wine—for the first time since the Middle Ages!

A   Vocabulary

1   Give the meaning of these expressions.
to blossom, it is not for nothing that, cider, densely, fertile, good husbandry, a pest, livestock, confined to, extensively, a yield, mainly, to eradicate, soil, output, market gardening
2   Give opposites of the following.
fertile, artificial, to diminish, mechanically, numerous

B   Questions on 'Agriculture in Britain'

1   What is the great enemy of hard fruits in Britain?
2   For what are many of the apples grown in the West of England used?
3   Are there only a few inhabitants per square kilometre in Britain?
4   Is agriculture of importance in Britain today?
5   Are more people than before the war employed in agriculture in Britain now?

6 What is barley used for?
7 How is most of the sugar crop harvested?
8 In what districts are sheep found?
9 Why is production per hectare high in Britain today?
10 For what are cattle bred in Britain?

C Grammar

1 Complete the following sentences with a present participle
or with an infinitive (the verb to use is given in brackets).

a We watched the man . . . . (dive), in a flash, into the sea.
b I heard a machine . . . . (thresh) the wheat in a nearby field.
c We saw the farmer's dog . . . . (jump) over the gate at once.
d I can smell something . . . . (burn) in the kitchen.
e She felt a spider . . . . (crawl) down her neck.
f We found the farmer . . . . (milk) the cows.
g Did you notice anyone . . . . (take) any money from this box?
h I heard Tom . . . . (shout) 'Take care!'
i We saw a ploughman . . . . (plod) behind his team of
horses.
j We left the culprits . . . . (look) very much ashamed of
themselves.
k We saw him . . . . (cut) the hedge.
l He left her . . . . (feel) very sorry for herself.
m We hoped that we would find him . . . . (cut) the grass in
front of his house.

2 Complete the following list.

Country	Person	Adjective	The people as a whole
England	an Englishman	English	the English
Poland			
Algeria			
Belgium			
Holland			
Sweden			
Mexico			
Portugal			
Greece			
Denmark			

3   Complete the following sentences.
   a Such crops as these need . . . .
   b Such a mistake as that means . . . .
   c Such men as Newton have helped . . . .
   d So sweet a smile as hers would charm . . . .
   e Such a story as that seems . . . .
   f He is such a good farmer that . . . .
   g There are so many pests in this region that . . . .
   h We produce such a lot of milk that . . . .
   i He is such a fine horse that . . . .
   j There are so many people in Britain that . . . .
   k The orchards are so beautiful that . . . .
   l The soil is so wet that . . . .
   m Those eggs are so good that . . . .
   n He has become so thin that . . . .
   o The winter is usually so mild that . . . .

D   Write an essay describing a farm that you know.

London is not Great Britain

About one eighth of the inhabitants of Great Britain live in the London area, and the head offices of a very large number of firms were established there, even though the factories may be in the provinces. It is this concentration of population and control that has given London an importance greater than even its area. Moreover, it is the city that is most visited by foreigners. This explains why London receives so much attention in a survey of Britain. However, it would be wrong to say that London is England.

People in the provinces not only have their own customs, dialects and manners but are also responsible for the greater part of British industrial production. For purposes of simplification, we may divide Britain into eight great industrial regions.

The Midland area around Birmingham and Wolverhampton produces vehicles, metal goods, electrical and engineering goods. In the near-by North Staffordshire area, around Stoke-on-Trent, we have 'The Potteries', where china and earthenware goods are made. This is also a coal-mining region.

In Yorkshire we find the woollen and worsted industry. Leeds is a great centre for clothing and engineering. Sheffield is famous for its steel and cutlery (the inter-city train from London was called 'The Master Cutler'). Hull is one of the most important fishing ports. The coal fields of southern Yorkshire extend down into the Midland area.

The cotton goods industry thrives in the mills of south-east Lancashire, with Manchester as its centre. Electrical goods, dye-stuffs and heavy engineering products are also made here. Liverpool is one of the world's great ports, where ship-repairing is carried out, and where new industries are now springing up.

South Wales is a coal-mining area, and today it is also important because factories producing plastics, chemicals, and textiles have recently been built, partly in order to prevent unemployment caused by the decrease in the labour force needed in the pits.

Coal is also mined in the eastern parts of Durham and Northumberland, where there is also an important iron and steel industry. Here too we find Britain's second most important shipbuilding and ship-repairing yards.

The most famous shipyards are further north, on Clydeside, just outside Glasgow, where there is also an extensive iron and steel industry. One of the main reasons for the industrial development

Steel working: molten iron ore gives out heat and sparks

of Britain lies in the fact that her coal and iron fields were close together, and this is true of the industrial belt of central Scotland, which extends from Glasgow to Edinburgh, for much coal is also mined in this area.

Northern Ireland is famed for its linen, but now also produces man-made fibres. Engineering is now of greater importance than ship-building. It is also a centre for the production of cigarettes and tobacco.

Finally, the London area is characterized by mixed light industry, by the concentration of business control already mentioned, and by its port.

The eight areas listed above are those with the greatest industrial output, though there is much industry elsewhere. Bristol, for instance, is a centre for the production of cigarettes and of aircraft engines. It is also an important industrial port. With the discovery of gas and oilfields in the North Sea, more remote parts of Britain are developing their own industry.

A   Vocabulary

1   What is meant by the following?
head office, a firm, the provinces, a dialect, earthenware, worsted, cutlery, a dyestuff, a pit, a labour force
2   What is the meaning of 'mills' in 'Industry thrives in the mills of Lancashire'?

B   Questions on 'London is not Great Britain'

1   Why is London so important?
2   Is industry in the provinces less important than that in the London area?
3   Where do we find the chief production of (a) woollen goods; (b) cotton goods; (c) coal?
4   Why are new industries to be found in South Wales?
5   For what is Hull famous?
6   What two raw materials are often found close together in Great Britain?
7   How many great industrial areas are there in Britain, apart from the London area?
8   In which parts of the country are Britain's greatest shipyards situated?
9   What goods do you think Britain might export to your country?
10   Give a list of goods that your country could export to Great Britain.

C Grammar

1 Give the verbs corresponding to the following nouns.
concentration, simplification, employment, decrease
(N.B. Where does the stress fall on this word?), production.

2 Give the past simple and the present and past participles of
these verbs.
find, thrive, spring, build, scatter

3 Give the plural of these words.
area, survey

4 Complete the following sentences.
a In order to . . . . , you should avoid the main roads.
b So that you . . . . , I will explain it in another way.
c To produce . . . . , we need more modern machinery.
d In order that our customers . . . . , we guarantee all our
goods for one year.
e So that our customers may know how to handle our
machines, we . . . .

D Write an essay on The distribution of industry in your own country.

Huddersfield, an industrial town in Yorkshire.